The Man Who
Amazed Atlanta

The Man Who Amazed Atlanta

The Journey of Franklin Miller Garrett

Franklin M. Garrett (signature)

Doris Lockerman

ATLANTA HISTORY CENTER
Atlanta, Georgia

and

LONGSTREET PRESS
Atlanta, Georgia

Published by
LONGSTREET PRESS, INC.
A subsidiary of Cox Newspapers,
A division of Cox Enterprises, Inc.
2140 Newmarket Parkway
Suite 118
Marietta, Georgia 30067

Printed in the United States of America

1st printing 1996

Library of Congress Catalog Card Number: 96-78834

ISBN: 1-56352-362-0

Jacket design by Laura McDonald
Book design and typesetting by Laura McDonald

*The publication of this book was made possible
by an anonymous gift from an admirer of Franklin Garrett.*

CONTENTS

Preface

Since his early manhood, Franklin Garrett has enjoyed a symbiotic relationship with professional word-and-fact users in Georgia—journalists, editors, media commentators, advertising account executives. He has been recognized as the source of accurate information about early and historic Atlanta and of its residents and events not available elsewhere. His cache of knowledge, gleaned through arduous searching over the years, has been generously shared without quibble or charge to anyone who has sought it.

"I always thought this was what it was for," he has said. "It wasn't cosmic news, of course, but it was important to those who needed it."

Against today's trumpeting of information as the driving, life-changing force of the age, Garrett's remarkable trove of footnoted historical publications and his instant recollection of the landscape of the Atlanta region have been recognized as intellectual property at its highest value.

For the greater part of his career, he has made his living working for business enterprises, quite apart from the accumulation of historical data. At the same time, he has developed a storehouse of facts that have become the foundation of the Atlanta Historical Society's ever-growing and remarkable archives.

Aside from that, almost every book of historical reference to Atlanta published in the last forty years has borne his imprimatur in a foreword comment, attesting to the authenticity of its contents. Feature articles for half a century have included the line "according to Franklin Garrett," as proof and appreciation.

He has, of course, never thought of using a press agent, nor arranging any publicity for his work. As a consequence, an unguarded reciprocity has sprung up between publishers and writers and Garrett. Hardly a week has passed that some writer or editor has not found a surprising new angle in Garrett's intellectual resource to share with readers or listeners.

This book is not intended to be a complete biography. It is an acknowledgment. Garrett is still at work, still achieving. He makes speeches every month to groups large and small, presides over and attends important meetings, ushers and greets at the First Presbyterian Church, advises other authors and commentators, reviews and revises manuscripts, and frequently receives yet another honor or award. Some of these honors have been awarded to him previously and are simply repeated, as emphasis.

Garrett drives to his snug, memento-filled office, where his secretarial colleague, Lil Salter, a wisp of observation and knowledge—comes in a few hours each day to type his printed notes and answer queries that come to the office each morning.

Mrs. Salter and Garrett had worked together at The Coca-Cola Company in former years. She knows Atlanta, as he does, by heart. Though Garrett has published millions of words, he does not type. He prints rapidly and legibly and has no use for any business machine whatever. His office does have a telephone that rings often. People ask for information. Real people, not "virtual" people. He gives them real answers.

The office also has a harmonica, a resident musical instrument, which Garrett picks up impulsively to blow an old sea chantey or a railroad lament for his amusement and Mrs. Salter's. It breaks the afternoon and lightens up the lower floor of the Atlanta Historical Society's McElreath Hall.

With the former Frances Steele Finney, his wife of eighteen years, he lives with comfort and satisfaction (often expressed) in a handsome classical house called Mainline (for his train passion), designed by the late architect Clement Ford to house the Garretts' fine collection of antiques, porcelains, paintings, crystal, and his impressive library, which is the second masterpiece achievement of Garrett's lifetime.

As a reminder of his longtime affair with railroading, Ford designed an indented tunnel niche down a long connecting hall between the two wings of the house, where a model train traverses its own track. Engineer Garrett is quick to point out that the train is a model, not a toy. (It is also a toy.)

As a lifetime writer, Garrett in his published works has a formal literary fluency, but years as a speaker on many platforms with many audiences have given him a conversational ease, along with free-ranging recollections.

This compilation is based on a series of taped reminiscences, unrehearsed and recorded, in his eighty-eighth and eighty-ninth years. They were conducted in one-hour sessions, and he used no notes whatever.

This is a tracing of Garrett's path and an identification of his remarkable points of arrival.

Acknowledgments

This book is about recognition, respect, kindness, attitude, and the value of small but significant events—all of utmost importance in a community.

Many people were sources for this reflection. Do you know . . . ? Has anyone told you . . . ? Remember the story . . . ? Oh, yes . . .

The reassuring encouragement of Louise Allen, the brightest strand in the fabric of the Atlanta Historical Society, and of Joseph W. Jones of The Coca-Cola Company was necessary for me to undertake this compilation. Their place in Atlanta is at the center of things.

Nor could it have been possible without Lil Salter, Franklin Garrett's aide-de-camp, and Frances Garrett, his wife and the center of his life.

On another plane, my gratitude to the firm of Rogers and Hardin for the discipline of technology in the final preparation of this manuscript.

Author's Note

Long before Cyberspace had been charted on planet earth, Atlanta's Franklin Miller Garrett had been functioning every day as the community's first Super Information Highwayman, using his remarkable brain and memory as software.

He had been called by many titles: Historian of the Atlanta Historical Society; Historian, City of Atlanta; Historian, County of Fulton. Also Mr. Atlanta, Mr. Grand Marshal, Mr. Total Recall, Mr. Foreword, Mr. Necrology, and, sometimes, Mr. Know-it-all. He answered to all of them with modesty.

Most recently, as he strode toward his ninetieth birthday, his portrait had been emblazoned on the side of a fifteen-story building, as one of Atlanta's Centennial Olympians. Garrett then heard a new title, gently voiced— Atlanta's treasure.

"Genius finds its own road and carries its own lamp."

— Wolmer

The Man Who
Amazed Atlanta

CHAPTER 1

1914

"Is Atlanta Always Like This, Papa?"

Over the years, Franklin Garrett has often said that his parents brought him to Atlanta as a lad of seven. Except for a few colorful memories, he has never dramatized his arrival in the South.

But to his parents, the family's arrival was no simple incident. They had spent several years testing other sections of the country, and Clarence Robert Garrett and his wife, Ada Katherine Garrett, had decided to trust their fortunes for the rest of their lives in Atlanta. Mr. Garrett had accepted a position as southeastern sales representative for the Morgan Millwork Company, with headquarters in Atlanta. He would be expected to cover his large territory by train.

Both of the elder Garretts had been born and reared in southern cities, Clarence in Richmond, where his father, William Franklin Garrett, had been a carpenter foreman of a planing mill. His mother was Cassie Miller Garrett, also of Richmond. Clarence Garrett's young wife had been born in Washington, D.C., on February 17, 1879, the daughter of Edwin Columbus Kirkwood and Alice Berry Kirkwood. Ada Kirkwood had been reared in both Washington and Baltimore.

Married, the young couple had tried their hands at opportunities in

Clarence Robert Garrett (1873–1946) and Ada Katherine Garrett (1879–1960), ca. 1905. Photo courtersy of Franklin M. Garrett

Milwaukee, Wisconsin, where young Franklin and his sister, Esther, were born. The family had later moved on to Grand Rapids, Michigan, and ultimately to Chicago for a few months before deciding to stake their future in Georgia.

Atlanta's strong reach for growth and progress had been trumpeted widely. Aside from its spectacular and devastating role in the Civil War, and its bitter experiences in the years of Reconstruction, Atlanta and its region had been publicized in the fiery speeches and editorials of the *Atlanta Constitution*'s dynamic Henry Grady. It was in 1884 that Grady had aroused the nation with his famous, conciliatory North-South speech in New York. After that time, two international expositions, both heavily advertised, and many convocations and conventions had spread Atlanta's promises far and wide.

In fact, the former Marthasville (as Atlanta had been known) had developed the art of self-promotion so energetically that its older and quieter neighboring cities often sniffed that "if Atlanta could inhale as well

Clarence Robert Garrett, ca. 1887. Photo courtesy of Franklin M. Garrett

*Franklin M. Garrett
and Esther
Kirkwood Garrett,
ca. 1912.*
Photo courtesy
of the Atlanta
History Center

*Franklin M.
Garrett, 1907.*
Photo courtesy of
Franklin M. Garrett

Henry Woodfin Grady (1851-1889).
Photo courtesy of the Atlanta History Center

as it exhales, we'd all be goners"—or in more earthly parlance, "If Atlanta could suck as hard as it blows, Lord help us all."

So it was no ordinary day, May 10, 1914, when the Garrett family disembarked from the Southern Railway's newest passenger train, the Royal Palm, at the city's fine new Terminal Station. The Royal Palm was a crack train that ran between Chicago and Florida.

The month of May was being its usual rapturous self. (The weather was still sullen and cold in Chicago.) A few white blossoms of dogwood still tilted in the soft air. Banners and flags fluttered in the breeze. Children laughed and played, and large men in exotic Arabian Nights costumes pranced and pranked on every side of the broad terminal plaza.

There was also music—the sounds of accordions, flutes, snare drums, even bells and fiddles—coming from unexpected bands of people. Determined music, all of it, strange and sure, affrighting the air.

The Garretts did not fit the celebrants. They were experienced trav-

Atlanta Terminal Station (1905-1971), 1908. Photo courtesy of the Atlanta History Center

Esther Kirkwood Garrett (1908–1975), 1918. Photo courtesy of Franklin M. Garrett

elers, and traveling, they knew, was serious business. They were respectably dressed. Father Garrett wore his three-piece suit, with vest carefully buttoned, and a dark felt hat. Mrs. Garrett wore a long, dark dress, a large, crowned hat, and, of course, soft cotton gloves. The children were in their Sunday best, Franklin in knickerbockers, long black stockings, and polished black shoes, with a cap seriously leveled on his forehead.

Little sister Esther, a sweet-faced five-year-old, bounced off the train in a fluffy skirt, her dark bangs almost hidden under a leghorn straw hat with a ribbon streamer. (There must have been a tiny bunch of starched violets somewhere in the trimming.) Esther's slippers were black Mary Janes, with flat heels. She walked carefully with her mother, holding her hand, skipping when she needed to keep up, following the men of the family into the merrymaking crowd.

Esther was about eighteen months younger than her brother. Garrett remembers her lovingly as a "very attractive girl. . . . I was very fond of

Peachtree Street looking north from the railroad viaduct during the Shriners' national convention, May 10-16, 1914. Photo courtesy of the Atlanta History Center

Shriners' parade south on Peachtree Street past the Candler Building, May 1914.
Photo courtesy of the Atlanta History Center

my sister. We were close all our lives."

The Shriners were in Atlanta for a three-day conclave, their first international convention in the South, and Atlanta was expecting them.

"I was aware of the excitement," Franklin recalls. "We all were. I asked my father, I think rather hopefully, 'Is Atlanta always like this?'"

Father Garrett answered slowly, "Well, no, son, I'm afraid it isn't."

But both children hoped the hullabaloo was in their honor anyway.

The *Atlanta Journal* of May 10, 1914, reflected on the occasion, and Franklin later reprinted the article in his epic *Atlanta and Environs* in 1954.

> Today and tomorrow the great company will grow by thousands instead of by dozens. Tonight the tom-toms and the gongs will be sounding. The hour is near for the gathering of the company.
>
> In the plain English of old Dan Webster, the Shriners are coming by trainloads today. Tonight they will have taken possession of Atlanta.

By tomorrow night the city's subjugation will be almost as complete as it was on a memorable occasion half a century ago when a gentleman in a blue uniform marched at the head of an army.

By Tuesday morning the plain ordinary Atlantan will be hard to find. It will look like all the world has turned Shriner.

For this Atlanta has been preparing for days, weeks, months, for a year. One year ago the plans were started. Months ago the hotels began to fill with reservations for the week starting May 10, 1914. It has been weeks since the decorators planned and began their work, and since the hotels, cafes, commission merchants and packing houses ordered their quantities of extra food and other supplies. Days ago Atlanta began to take on a festive air, an attitude of anticipation.

Now the city is ready for the Shriners. And now the Shriners are about to get here. Some of them have been on their way for days. Four trainloads of Californians left their homes two weeks ago. They got here this afternoon. Other trainloads from the far northwest, the southwest, from upper Canada, started a week or more ago. They are drawing near now. Tomorrow three times as many as came today will get here.

Patrols and bands will be marching today from stations to hotels and back again, and countermarching through the streets and serenading Atlanta and each other as the whim strikes them. . . .

Thousands of visiting Shriners were accommodated in the Southern Railway's 'Shrine Park' in the railroad's yards at North Avenue and Marietta Street. Here 150 Pullman cars were parked, elaborately decorated and brilliantly illuminated.

——— — ———

The *Journal* continued:

With all her buildings gaily decorated from casement to roof and with every resident ready to extend cordial greetings to the thousands of Shriners who are to make merry here this week, Atlanta is in a carnival mood. The next four days will be one continuous round of festivities, for Atlanta is determined that all who come this week shall go back to their scattered homes tired but happy and ready to swear that they have had the 'time of their lives.'

Balls, receptions, races, exhibition drills, open-air dancing, garden parties, southern suppers, everything that the heart and brain of hospitable local Shriners could devise will contribute to the gaiety of the week, while the visitors themselves will augment the pace by entertainments of their own.

The crescent, star and scimitar will rule the city and to every wearer of the fez will be accorded the hand of friendship and good fellowship. At all the entertainments formalities will be eliminated.

——— — ———

So the Shriners and the Garretts came to Atlanta the same week.

Hotel rooms, of course, were impossible to find. The newcomers had not realized that would be a problem in blustering Atlanta.

But the Garretts were resourceful. They remembered that they had a cousinly kinsman in Atlanta, an older man who had left Richmond for Georgia and had long ago made his mark in Atlanta. His name was George E. Johnson, and he had just been elected judge of the Recorder's Court in Fulton County.

Judge Johnson knew everyone, and everyone knew him. He was exactly the right man for networking, an old accepted custom in Dixie and its environs. Judge Johnson found a place for them to stay until they could find a permanent home.

The hotel was called the Peachtree Inn, Franklin recalls. "It had formerly been known as the Alhambra. It had been built to take up some of the overflow of traffic from the Exposition of 1895."

It took no time to find out that their relative was popular.

The *Atlanta Journal* noted Judge Johnson's first day on the bench at the police station:

The new recorder was no stranger to local law enforcement circles. For he had, in former years, rendered valiant service as a police commissioner. For 26 years he was a candy manufacturer and in this connection his generosity will be long remembered. Every Christmas he extended a blanket invitation to all the poor children in the city to come to his place for a Santa Claus bag of candy. And though they came by the hundreds, none were sent away empty handed. In 1886, Judge Johnson was married to Miss Eleanor Morgan, daughter of David Morgan, a pioneer Atlanta harness manufacturer.

Fines and fun, sternness and shrewdness, mirth and mercy in equal mixtures marked the new recorder's first day on the job. His first fine was $10.75 for reckless driving, his first bond was $500 for larceny, his first dismissal was an old Negro well-digger, his first innovation was that of swearing in defendants in every case.

——— — ———

The Garretts could stay at the Peachtree Inn for only a few days, but already Franklin had learned about freedom in a smaller town. His father permitted him to walk up and down the street as long as he didn't get into traffic.

"There were two buildings that attracted my attention," Franklin remembers. "One was very ornate, a two-and-a-half story or three-story Victorian brick house at the corner of Peachtree and Currier, which I soon learned was the old Marion C. Kiser home. Kiser was a wealthy man, who, when he died in 1893, had left the largest estate that Fulton County had ever administered at that time. Of course, I learned all that much later, but this house impressed me as a little boy, with all its turrets, etc."

So Franklin had started noticing. Noticing was to be his destiny.

——— — ———

Garrett was thinking back eighty years or so.

"I was telling you about the first homes I had observed. You know we had stopped as transients at the Peachtree Inn, next door to St. Luke's Episcopal Church, which was very new then.

"The other house at the opposite end of the block, to the south of Peachtree and Pine Street, was the original Grant home . . . grandmother of the Grant who built the place on Paces Ferry now owned by the Cherokee Club. . . . That building was red brick, half brown, I guess.

"The house was surrounded by wrought-iron fence. There was a fountain in the front yard. That fountain today is on the grounds of the Historical Society at the north entrance to the Swan House, where the deliveries are made. A beautiful fountain. It was moved from the Grant place at Peachtree and Pine around to the John W. Grant home on Paces Ferry and the Historical Society acquired it. It had a servants' and carriage house on the back on Pine Street. Over the door was a marble date stone . . . 1874. That impressed me tremendously. I began looking for dates on other buildings."

About ten days later, when the Garretts had found a home and taken possession of an almost new duplex at 68 Thirteenth Street, between Peachtree and Piedmont, the family felt they had put down permanent

John T. Grant residence, 319 Peachtree Street, 1881. Photo courtesy of the Atlanta History Center

roots. They felt free to let their inquisitive little son look around the neighborhood.

The memories of Chicago, with its winters and delivery wagons drawn by great draft horses, began to fade. One of Franklin's favorite places in Chicago, Marshall Fields, became a happy memory.

"I think Marshall Fields was built the same year I was born. I'm not sure which has lasted better! They had wonderful trains in the toy department."

He was never to lose his interest in trains. "Trains have always fascinated me. I really got more interested in them in Chicago, which was the railroad center of the United States. That was when steam was the power. It was before diesels came in . . . and while diesels are more efficient, they lack the romance of the steam locomotive . . . the sounds they make, with everything working so you can see it. No, I have never lost interest in trains."

But other things were happening in Atlanta and the South.

Three months after the Garretts arrived in Atlanta, the United States was only one year away from the onset of World War I, already smoldering for many months in Europe. When World War I broke in August, touched off by the assassination of Archduke Ferdinand in Sarajevo, all the major cotton exchanges in the South were closed.

In May, when the Shriners had frolicked on Peachtree Street, middling cotton was being sold at twelve cents a pound. By fall, there would be no market. The economic gears of the South were quickly becoming unmeshed, and "the specter of bankruptcy and suffering stalked the old red hills of Georgia."

During the following weeks bales of cotton began to appear in bank and hotel lobbies as part of a "buy a bale" movement, and in October 1914, Atlanta's wealthiest citizen, Asa G. Candler, announced his own plan to save Georgia's farmers.

Headlined in the *Atlanta Journal* on October 14:

ASA G. CANDLER TO LEND $30,000,000 ON COTTON. BASIS IS SIX CENTS, LOANS WILL RUN UNTIL JULY 1915.

Storage for several thousand bales will be ready by October 24. Additional space will be provided as required. We believe that after it is demonstrated that a normal crop will not be planted next year, cotton will advance to a fair price.

The offer was backed by the Central Bank and Trust Corporation, of which Mr. Candler was president.

The newcoming Garretts, of course, had not expected any of this, neither the Shriners nor the impending economic debacle. But to rise above disaster had been Atlanta's genius and its history, and just now there was much to rise above.

The most infamous criminal case in southern memory had just concluded with a shameful lynching. The dreadful Leo Frank case, never to be forgotten in judicial or social history, was indelibly imprinted on the soul of the South.

Clarence and Ada Garrett were quiet, thoughtful parents who controlled

Asa Candler (seated center) at the army barracks at Camp Gordon, 1918. Photo courtesy of the Atlanta History Center

their young son and little daughter with gentle persuasion. Later in his life, Franklin could recall only one time his father lifted a hand to him in punishment. "My father struck me only once . . . probably a push on the arm, which I know I deserved."

Esther was too young for school, but Franklin was enrolled at the Tenth Street School, which all the children in his new neighborhood attended. It was only a skip and a jump from Piedmont Park, a historic green space then bursting with the exuberance of summer in the South. As a second grader going on eight years old, Franklin set out to investigate his environs, which, of course, began his life's career.

His peregrinations became bolder. His new neighbors observed him: a sturdy, self-possessed boy remarking on every landmark in the community, noticing street names, house numbers, the architecture of buildings, every tree, hill, creek, and animal in sight. He also learned the names of residents and gradually got acquainted with everybody living nearby.

Four streetcar lines radiated out into growing Atlanta near the Garretts' residence. Franklin was permitted to ride them when he had the time, to the very end of each line and back, missing nothing. He was interest-

Tenth Street School, 1905. Photo courtesy of the Atlanta History Center

ed in destinations, for whom streets were named, houses, their history and structures, old and new.

He had become an avid reader. He had soon read all the well-known boys' books—*Tom Swift, Boy Allies, The Rover Boys,* and *Putnam Hall Cadets.*

He always liked to acquire complete sets of books. And he learned early to be careful about who borrowed them from him.

"Of course I've made exceptions all my life, but I would really rather buy a new copy of a favorite book than get it back with a ruined binding. I had one friend place a flowerpot on one of my favorite books, for example. I never forgot that. I value my books very highly."

Father Garrett was often away on business, calling on his customers all over the Southeast. Mrs. Garrett supervised the home and family. Franklin's father had the genial personality of a natural salesman. A man of small stature, he had a surprising streak of boyish gaiety that led him to indulge in sudden dances and games when the family was at leisure. "I think they call what he did clap dancing. . . . I always admired it."

Franklin himself has been known to break into railroad chanteys and quirky melodies at unexpected moments, and his bass-baritone voice has been caught on radio waves singing some little ditty.

"As I think I told you before, I lived close to Piedmont Park. I had many happy days playing there. We had a game called Fox and Hounds, or Ditching, as we called it. Say there were eight boys. They would form two sides with four boys each. One of each side would be allowed to disappear. The other team was allowed to catch them. If you could catch one of them and could hold one of them long enough to say 'Willow Willow Wee,' that boy was out of the game.

"A fascinating section of Piedmont Park was called the Bridle Path. You got into it where they had a barn to keep the equipment. The Bridle Path ran across Clear Creek, which was the official name of it, and ran down almost to Piedmont where the railroad made a loop. You see, the eastern part of the park was undeveloped at the time we took up residence. The creek really started at Tenth Street and meandered north and finally flowed into Peachtree Creek out there at Armour Sta-

Franklin M. Garrett, 1916. Photo courtesy of the Atlanta History Center

tion, beyond the Seaboard railroad tracks.

"The boys on Thirteenth Street used to visit the Swingin' Bridge, which had been built across a swamp down at Armour Station, about one mile down the railroad from Brookwood Station. So the Thirteenth Street boys . . . the Donaldson boys and the Douglass boys, would often gather and someone would say, 'Let's go up to the Swingin' Bridge,' because you could get on it and swing up and down. It was built by the Georgia Power Company for a transmission line across this swamp. We had a lot of fun doing that.

"Of course in getting out there . . . that was where the Southern Railway was, you could see passenger trains going by. We all liked trains, as you know, as I still do. At Piedmont Park, the Southern Railway Belt Line, which, back in the early years of this century, was the main line of the Southern Railroad coming in from Charlotte and Washington . . . went to DeKalb Avenue, where it paralleled the Georgia Railroad down to the old Union Station. That was of great interest to me. Many times I awoke at night to hear a steam locomotive over there with a long string of cars . . . pulling hard . . . upgrade. . . . I can hear it now. . . .

"Tenth Street Elementary School was only a nice little walk, about three blocks from my home, but boys are always boys and we wouldn't all go the same way. We'd look for shortcuts. I remember there was a rather caustic lady, a Mrs. Gachet, who lived on Twelfth Street by herself. She didn't like boys walking across her yard. She would come out of her house and order us off every now and then. But we had other routes . . . Piedmont Avenue, sometimes Peachtree Street, and the alleys in between.

"Lots of times we'd cut across the Ansley Golf Club, which was not pleasing to the golfers. I remember that the golf club was bordered by Collier Woods, and it was really woods. The only house there was the Wash Collier home, which is now occupied by Jimmy Bentley and his family. The Bentleys made a lot of improvements, but, as a matter of fact, the house had previously been greatly improved by an architect named Cannon Perry.

"Cannon Perry didn't live in it too long before he died. I'm not sure that Bentley didn't buy it from his heirs or estate. Anyhow, the Colliers didn't really like visitors, and we tried to avoid the house, but I remem-

John T. Thrashe (1818-1899), George W. Collier (1813-1903), and George W. Adair (1823-1899) in Collier Woods, 1897. Photo courtesy of the Atlanta History Center

ber one time a golfer at the Ansley Club made a poor shot of some sort. The boys kinda laughed at him. He had just dug up a lot of ground. He got mad and threw his club at us. . . . We were between him and Collier Woods. The club went over into the woods. I think he may have found it. Anyway, we ceased to cross the golf club after that.

"I think all the boys I knew as a youth are gone. The Donaldson boys are gone. Rutledge Beauchamp is gone. Raymond Bowles is gone. Of course, as in all neighborhoods, the families came and went and it wasn't always the same boys playing together."

CHAPTER 2

1917

World War I — "Against Eternal Wrong"

When Franklin was eleven, word was received from Washington, D.C., that Atlanta had definitely been selected as a cantonment site and that it would be named Camp John B. Gordon, in honor of the late, distinguished Confederate general and Georgia governor and senator. Meanwhile, Atlanta had also been selected as southeastern headquarters of the American Red Cross, and on April 6, 1917, came the announcement everybody had been expecting: "U.S. IS NOW AT WAR."

Said the *Atlanta Journal* editorial that day: "The war with Germany is on, a war of democracy against despotism, of civilization against slavery, of eternal right against eternal wrong, a war in which, as the President declared, 'America is privileged to spend her blood and her might for the principles that gave her birth and happiness and the peace which she has treasured.'"

A few days later, word was received that Fort McPherson had been selected as one of the fourteen sites in the country for the training of applicants for commissions. A couple of days later, ten contractors and one thousand workmen were busy on the grounds erecting new wooden barracks and other necessary buildings. Less than a month later, the first contingent of officers-to-be arrived at the fort.

The urgent need for food crops turned weeded and vacant lots all over town into vegetable gardens. Sixty-five acres of city-owned land were soon under cultivation. At Maddox Park, eleven acres of corn, a half acre of carrots, and one and a half acres of Irish potatoes were underway; at Mozley Park, nine and a half acres of miscellaneous vegetables; at Piedmont Park, five acres of corn; and at the stockyard, some fifty acres of grains and vegetables.

Franklin's parents had decided to attend the handsome new First Church of Christ, Scientist, built only a year earlier (and still one of Atlanta's most admired structures). The children were entered in the church's Sunday school.

But the quiet religious climate of Atlanta exploded with the announcement on November 3, 1917, that William Ashley "Billy" Sunday, an ordained Presbyterian minister, would arrive in Atlanta for a stay of several weeks to preach his electrifying message to the South.

"I expect Atlanta to come to the plate and line them out so fast that the devil himself will have his tongue hanging out, and when the game is called, the score will be one of which Atlanta will be proud. Time has come to clear the decks for action, to come out of the trenches and go over the top for God, home and native land."

Everyone turned out to hear the fire-and-brimstone evangelist. Society leaders, the governor, the mayor, opera fiends, fight fans, and churchmen mingled in the vast crowd of revival goers.

Ward Green wrote in the *Atlanta Journal* the next day:

> On his first day in the South Billy Sunday has taken off his coat to Atlanta. He has preached three typical sermons at the Jackson Street Tabernacle. He has leaped and crawled and bounded and strutted himself into a knot, and pegged the declamatory ball into deep center to the home plate. Something like 30,000 people have heard him and these he has interested, amused, delighted, disgusted, shocked, thrilled and exhilarated, each according to his bent.
>
> 'O God!' pleaded Billy Sunday. 'If this city of Atlanta, pearl

of the South, will fall on her knees before you and come over to Christ, then I say that this whole southland, drenched in tears of repentance, will do as Atlanta does. Men and women of Atlanta, I hold before you the bleeding form of Jesus Christ. Take Him if you will!'

It went on for seven weeks. It was one of Atlanta's great emotional experiences.

————— — —————

When Billy Sunday departed, John McCormack, the great Irish tenor, came to Atlanta and sang a program of intimate, soothing, sentimental songs to an audience of five thousand on November 19, 1917. He sang "Little Mother O' Mine," "My Little Gray Home in the West," "Mother Machree," and "Keep the Home Fires Burning."

"There were tears in a thousand eyes at the last, which came as the final song of the evening."

————— — —————

December 1917 was termed the coldest December in the history of the city. A strange experience was in store for Atlantans.

"Out at Piedmont Park the glimmering surface of a once-liquid lake presented a sight which made onlookers doubt their sobriety. Strange hieroglyphics were being carved in the winter air by figures that curved and shot and reached amazing momentum on skates. It sounds like a dream, but it actually happened. Lowry Arnold, Philip L'Engle, Arthur Clarke, and sundry others of Atlanta's prominent gentry disported themselves artistically and hilariously on water which had met a hard fate." Garrett himself observed this and reported it again thirty-four years later in his book *Atlanta and Environs*.

————— — —————

But by the summer of 1917, work on the construction of Camp Gordon was going full blast. Noted Garrett later, from a news report of the time:

A little over a month ago twelve miles from Atlanta there is a section of land containing many acres. It looked the same as the thousands of other rolling areas that surrounded it. Today there is a different picture to be seen. Cornfields have given way to barracks that will shelter Uncle Sam's fighting men, roads have been cut through the hills, spur railroad tracks have been laid, trees have been felled, to make way for barracks and messhalls, and 4,000 workmen are now engaged in building an army city that soon will be the temporary home of 40,000 or more young Americans, assembled there to be trained for the European battlefields.

The place was the Gordon cantonment—Camp Gordon.

About a year later, on September 25, 1918, Franklin's parents gave him exactly what he had longed for, a Niagara bike with a Morrow coaster brake, with no gadgets on the handlebars and no fancy equipment . . . a bike that he could ride long distances, not just on the sidewalks around his home.

"My first ride was to Camp Gordon. You see, World War I was still going on and the camp at Chamblee was going full blast. It ended a couple of months later, on November 11, 1918, of course.

"I had heard a lot about Camp Gordon and wondered what it looked like, but I had no way of getting there until I got my bicycle.

"It was a straight shot out Peachtree. About twelve miles to the north. It was at Chamblee, as you may know, on the east side of the railroad tracks, across from the business area of Chamblee. At that time the pavement ended at the DeKalb County line, which was where Club Drive goes off. I rode out to Camp Gordon and looked it over. I was very impressed. The streetcar had been extended out there in 1917, but I had ridden my own wheels."

CHAPTER 3

1920

Young Garrett Gets His Wish — An Encyclopedia

By 1920, although he professed to be only an average grammar school student, it was obvious that the fourteen-year-old Garrett's interest in history and geography was far superior to the aspirations of his teenage friends. He had shown little ability in mathematics, but assiduously devoured current events in daily journals and had read everything he could find about ancient as well as modern general history.

His reach in scholarship had already far exceeded his parents' grasp, but they tried hard to facilitate his intellectual direction. Self-determined he had proved to be, but they would not let it appear that he also had been self-made. They provided whatever tools they could afford to further his progress.

For his fourteenth birthday, Franklin requested Ridpath's *Encyclopedia of Universal History*, the work of John Clark Ridpath, LL.D., who had also published monographs on monetary developments.

The four-volume encyclopedia, sold by subscription only and ordered in advance, was to be Franklin's belated birthday and Christmas present, the only gift he would hope for.

The first volume ran to 680 pages. It covered Oriental monarchies and the Hellenic ascendencies, and explained that the material had been written somewhat less formally than other works of its kind, which are "elaborate in detail and so recondite in method that the common reader has neither courage to undertake, nor time to complete them. Before a single topic can be mastered he finds himself lost in a labyrinth."

The fourth volume opened with an engraving of Abraham Lincoln and concentrated on the history of the United States, which "shall join in glad acclaim to usher in the golden age of humanity and the universal monarchy of men."

Ridpath's was the first important acquisition in Garrett's personal library; it has never stopped growing and has long since been one of the finest private library collections in the region. Inscribed by a strong boy's hand, "Franklin M. Garrett, 1920," the encyclopedia is immaculate and pristinely bound, and Garrett values it beyond price.

——— — ———

High schools in Atlanta were not coeducational when Franklin graduated from grammar school. Most of his friends chose to go to Tech High and so, notwithstanding his distaste for math and sciences, he entered the technical high school along with them.

Franklin says he never was an athlete. "Football never interested me much and basketball less. I liked baseball better . . . played it better, but all I ever really played was sandlot baseball. My athletic experience was pretty limited. I played on the dodgeball team, the potato-relay team, and the volleyball team. I enjoyed that in grammar school, but I was never involved in athletics after I got to high school.

"One of the reasons I wasn't was that I began my high school education when old Tech High was on Luckie Street and Marietta Street. Incidentally, the building is still standing. It is painted pink now, and it is the Phoenix Dance Club. (I'm sure Dr. Sutton and Dr. Cheney would probably turn over in their graves. Their offices, I believe, were in the main building.)

"Anyway, I got a high school education at Tech High that I considered adequate. When I started there in 1920, a good many of the students were considerably older. Some of them were four or five years

Atlanta Technical High School–Atlanta Boys High School basketball game, ca. 1919.
Photo courtesy of the Atlanta History Center

older, because their education had been interrupted by World War I, when they went into the service, and they entered high school when they came back.

"I remember our football team at Tech High was college age . . . that was my first year there, but I never went out for any athletics. . . . I just wasn't too steamed up over that.

"Tech High was good for boys who were going to use math in their careers. Well, I got by, but I didn't do too well in that subject. My interests were in history, literature, geography, and such subjects.

"I started to work as soon as I could. My first steady job was during the summer vacations, the summers of 1921, '22 and '23. At that time Peachtree and Tenth Street was the place the neighborhood boys gathered. It was a retail center, individually owned stores, grocery stores, drugstores, Taylor Brothers, Marshall Pharmacy, and one that eventually became Lane Drugs.

"I hired out as a delivery boy for the Marshall Drug Store. The pay was a neat $10 a week. Marshall was a good man to work for. We used our bicycles to deliver orders. I wasn't the only one, of course. There were three of us, as I remember. There was Harvey Hunter . . . Red Hunter, we called him, who lived on Juniper Street, Donald Armstrong, who later became the head man of the Crane Company here in Atlanta. The other one was Malon Courts. Malon lived almost next door to the drugstore in an apartment on the west side of Peachtree and Tenth Streets. They were big apartments, as I remember them.

"The Courts family had come to Atlanta in 1909, I think. Mr. Courts was the traveling freight agent for the Illinois Central Railroad. I went to Tenth Street School with their three children.

"Richard W. was the eldest. He died in 1993. He was a very handsome man and a good businessman. He married Miss Virginia Campbell, the only daughter of Mr. and Mrs. Bulow Campbell. Mrs. Bulow Campbell was the former Laura Berry, sister of Miss Martha Berry, who founded the Berry School in Rome, Georgia.

"Richard was ten years my senior, so as a boy, I was not his contemporary.

"The third child was Virginia. She and I were born the same year. I thought she was a beautiful girl. She married quite young, a man named Tucker Wayne. He was a good man, owned an advertising agency. Tucker Wayne was in an automobile accident on Habersham Road and died in 1962, leaving her a widow. They had only one child, a daughter named Mary, who is now Mrs. William Dixon.

"I always liked Virginia. I had a date or two with her before she married Tucker, and after Tucker died, I began to date her. We enjoyed each other's company. We went to the Piedmont Ball and affairs like that. She was a good dancer . . . anybody could dance well with her.

"Malon was born in 1908 and in due course married Vaughn Nixon. Vaughn's father owned and managed the Atlanta Woolen Mills. Vaughn and Malon Courts were the handsomest couple in Atlanta, many people agreed.

"They were married and devoted to each other. Malon developed some kind of heart trouble. He was a great tennis player. So was his brother, Richard. Incidentally, when Richard died in 1993, he held the oldest membership in the Driving Club.

"The doctors told Malon he was going to have to quit playing tennis. Well, he couldn't quit. In the summer of 1967, he was playing tennis with Bill Nixon, his wife's brother. Malon went into the locker room after a game and died suddenly before anybody could do anything.

"Malon and his brother, Richard, were a perfect pair to operate Courts and Company, their brokerage business. I think their father founded it, but the sons were moving spirits, too. As reserved as Richard was, Malon was outgoing . . . made friends easily. Now they are all gone . . . the three Courts children.

"Well, back to Marshall's Drug Store. It was open until eleven o'clock every night, and we rotated between day and night shifts. I learned all about Ansley Park making deliveries because so many of Marshall's customers lived there. I know Ansley Park so well now I could go around it in the dark. It is the best close-in community of Atlanta, I think. But when I was a boy it was way out north of the city limits.

"We also had one black delivery man, who delivered for Marshall's going further out."

——— — ———

"I graduated from Tech High in 1924. At that time we were living at 822 Penn Avenue. I had some good friends there, like the Norcross family and the Norris family across the street. The Bridges family lived at Seventh Street. Miss Berman lived there, too . . . my first-grade teacher, Miss Rosa Berman. And the Kurtz family. Wilbur Kurtz, Sr., was old enough to be my father . . . but we were good friends. We were both interested in the city of Atlanta and its history.

CHAPTER 4

A Close Family with a Light Rein and Their Neighbors

Clarence and Ada Garrett, quiet, thoughtful, and unpretentious, were apparently exactly the right parents for their talented and creative children. Guiding them with a light rein, they apparently were successful in supporting, not stifling, the personalities and natural abilities of both Franklin and his admirable sister.

"We had a very pleasant home, comfortable. My father was away a great deal in his work, and toward the end of his life he was often not very well. He had only a limited interest in history, and my mother only a little more. But no, they never gave me any flak about wasting my time prying into the past, as some parents would have."

Esther, a bright, active girl, had a high achievement record in both Girls High and Washington Seminary. She was a top student in her grammar grades and a star basketball guard in high school. Her school scrapbook, still in her brother's possession, was filled with dance cards, invitations, bridge tallies, snapshots, and amusing recollections of class outings.

After high school, Esther went to work for the Retail Credit Company (now Equifax), and in 1930, when she was twenty-two, she married William Lovejoy Harwell of Decatur, son of Judge and Mrs. Frank Harwell. Esther had to leave Retail Credit when she married Lovejoy because the Woolford men, who were the original founders of Retail Credit, did not believe that married women should keep jobs that men could fill.

She was very active in garden clubs and civic organizations, including historic preservation groups, and had a long service with the American Red Cross.

Divorced from Lovejoy Harwell in 1935, Esther was sent to Europe as director of clubs for the American Red Cross early in World War II. Franklin's files include a snapshot of a slender, young Esther in Red Cross uniform at a microphone in Sardinia, Italy, during a military celebration. Her résumé of activities, both as a young girl and as a matron, was long and impressive, especially in Savannah.

Back in Atlanta, she married Lamar (Red) Wynne, and they established their home in Savannah. After working in real estate sales for a while, Esther set up her own business, the Esther G. Wynne Real Estate Company, specializing in historic Savannah residences primarily between Gaston Street and the Savannah River.

Mr. and Mrs. Garrett, Franklin's parents, were living in an apartment at Piedmont and Eighth Street in 1946 when another apartment in the building caught fire, sending smoke to the Garrett suite. Franklin obtained temporary refuge for them in the Georgian Terrace Hotel. Garrett, Sr., died there in March 1946. He had not been well. His death was apparently not considered related to the apartment fire. Mrs. Garrett later moved to Savannah to reside with her daughter and her husband. She died there in 1960.

Esther Garrett Wynne had built up a very nice business when she died suddenly in 1975. Her death was a special shock. Her husband had gone to the hospital with a mild heart attack, and when she went to see him, she suffered a heart attack herself. She died in the hospital in July 1975. She was sixty-seven years old.

"I still miss Esther," Garrett said. "We were always very close."

During Esther's life, Franklin went to Savannah frequently to visit the Wynnes and his mother, invariably taking the Nancy Hanks Central of Georgia train, which was a pleasure for him to ride.

"Amtrak discontinued it. . . . They never had operated it and so most of my trips to Savannah after that were by automobile. I went through the towns of Eatonton and Watkinsville, which were more interesting to me than the freeway any day of the week."

———— — ————

Young Franklin always knew that his neighbors were important. "I knew their names. I considered them pleasant friends and always have.

"Before we go on, I want to tell you about them.

"The street north of us was Fourteenth. Now Fourteenth Street was more highly rated as a residential street than either Twelfth or Thirteenth. And many well-known families were living in that block, between Peachtree and Piedmont.

"On the northeast corner was the great Murphy estate, where Colony Square is now. Then, coming down Fourteenth Street, on the north side of the street, the first house was the Loyless home, where Mr. and Mrs. Augustus Loyless lived. He published a trade magazine for the soft drink industry, I believe. They had one son, Augustus. Augustus married Helen Bivings. She had a brother named Troy who died young. The next house was a brick residence, the W. S. Duncan home. He was a wholesale hay, feed, and grain dealer, and apparently did very well. Next was the Evins home. The older son was Elliott Evins. He had a high-pitched voice. When he walked, he walked on his tiptoes.

"There was the Harrison Jones family and then a three-story apartment in which the Nixon family lived. They had three children. Bill, who was my age, had a hot temper. I remember when we were playing sandlot baseball, if Bill struck out, he'd throw down his bat. Emmy, the daughter—married Bill Parker—I admired them both very much. The Parkers lived next door to the Nixons. The Nixons also had a young daughter named Vaughn to whom I have already referred. She married Malon Courts.

"Next door to the Parkers was the home of Harrison Jones, who became one of the top officers of The Coca-Cola Company.

"Then the Collings family. They had a son named Dave.

"Then there was a house where one of the daughters of Laurent

DeGive married and lived. It was a square house with a white exterior. This was quite a house.

"There was a vacant lot, no . . . there was one house, right across Pause Street, a stone house where the Peeples family lived. Robyn grew up there and her brother as well. Pause Street was named for a restaurant owner, I think. That street name has been changed.

"On the south side of Fourteenth Street, coming down from Peachtree, lived the Gilbert family, including sons Price and Francis. Francis had become bald-headed early in life and was nicknamed Cueball. Cueball Gilbert died young. Price was the older son. Their father was a judge of the Supreme Court of Georgia. Price Gilbert went to The Coca-Cola Company early on. He ended up owning a good deal of Coca-Cola stock, which I think went to Georgia Tech, because the library there is named for him. Price never married. He was a wealthy Atlanta bachelor.

"We lived on Thirteenth Street. There were four streetcar lines within a block: the Brookwood line, which terminated at Piedmont Avenue; the Peachtree/Brookwood line, which ran out to Brookwood Station; the Courtland/Juniper line, which terminated at Thirteenth and Piedmont Avenue; and the Park Lane line, which ran out to Piedmont Park and then back to the city. They all had destinations on the other side of town. One was the Walker/Westview line, the other the Washington/Lakewood line.

"On Thirteenth Street was a diversified group, to say the least. Thirteenth Street at that time was a duke's mixture of houses. Near Peachtree and where Thirteenth Street runs off Peachtree—you remember the Peachtree Arts Theatre was there at one time on the northeast corner.

"On the southeast corner was the A. J. Orme home. The Ormes had three daughters, Sarah, Callie, and Cornelia, and one son, Quill, who married one of the Dodd girls. Let's see, there were Julia, Dorothy, and Nellie Dodd. Quill married Nellie Dodd. Quill died at an early age. Nellie survived him by a long time.

"The Ormes' daughter Sarah is a mighty fine person. She was born in 1902. She married William E. Huger. She tells the story that when one of their children was graduating from E. Rivers School, the very dignified principal handing out the diplomas came to Callie and said, 'And now, Miss Callie Hugger.' That greatly amused and embarrassed the family.

"Mr. Huger was a native of Charleston, and his business connection was with Courts and Company.

"Sarah has been a widow for several years . . . lived for many years on Valley Road, but has now been at Lenbrook for some time.

"The other two daughters, Callie and Cornelia, married the Healey brothers. Cornelia married Oliver Healey, and Callie married Bill Healey. Cornelia is deceased, and Oliver died recently. Bill Healey is deceased, too. Callie lives at Lenbrook, sure does. They were on that corner.

"On the other corner, where the theater was, was the home of Dr. Dunbar Roy, of a fairly old Atlanta family. I always admired that house; I remember it was just the right shade of red. Then back of those houses was an alley that ran through from Twelfth to Fourteenth Streets. On the Thirteenth Street alley was an ice house. The Atlantic Ice and Coal Company had houses around town where you could go and buy a block of ice for your icebox. That was known as the Ice Alley.

"Then everything east of that facing Thirteenth Street were single houses. I don't think there was an apartment there.

"When we first settled in, the first house we lived in was a duplex. Next door was a vacant lot where the boys played baseball. Every now and then they'd knock a ball over and break a basement window in the house we lived in.

"The first house on the right on Thirteenth Street was a gingerbread house occupied by Mr. Silas H. Donaldson. Mr. Donaldson was connected with the Fulton County Convict System. His older brother, Thomas J. Donaldson, lived on Peachtree Street in a big, old frame house painted dark green. He was superintendent of the Fulton County Convict System. And they didn't take any guff off the convicts. The convicts used to say, 'Cap'n Tom and Cap'n Si . . . If they don't kill you you'll never die.'

"The Donaldsons were fairly prolific on children. Silas and Reuben, the other brother . . . Reuben Donaldson lived on Twelfth Street and the Car Alley. Now the Car Alley extended on the block between Twelfth and Thirteenth Streets. It served the Courtland/Juniper streetcar line, which terminated at Thirteenth Street.

"The Car Alley was a single track—a double track after it got to Juniper Street. That was the streetcar line my mother rode going downtown to shop. Reuben Donaldson was a contractor, and his home stood until very recently at Twelfth and the Car Alley. . . . So there were three sets of Donaldson boys.

"Thomas J. Donaldson, his oldest child was Clark Donaldson, who became head of the city construction division . . . a good citizen. Then the next son was Thomas J., Jr., who was a clerk at the Atlanta Freight Terminal, where the Georgia Freight Depot is now. I didn't know any of them because they were old enough to be my father. Then came . . . as far as boys were concerned . . . Thomas, Jr., Smith, and then Jasper, who was a good friend of mine. I was one of his pallbearers when he died. Jasper was business manager for years for the Atlanta Crackers. I always liked Jasper. He was a good athlete, even though he was of small stature. He was a baseball player and an associate of Earl Mann, who headed the Crackers. Jasper was the business manager. They traveled around the South playing ball. Jasper, Thomas, and Smith made extra money during the summer being lifeguards at Piedmont Park swimming pool and lake. They were experts at a rowboat. . . . They just sat there in the rowboat . . . but they were alert . . . in case anybody was about to drown. Incidentally, nobody did . . . accidentally, anyway.

"Now Silas H. Donaldson—these three brothers were sons of the senior Silas H. Donaldson—owned a good bit of land in what would now be the intersection of Blackland Road, Powers Ferry Road, and Roswell Road. He came into this very early, before the Civil War.

"Si's children were all boys. There were Fred, Horace, Tick, and Tom Q. (called T. Q.). Fred, Horace, Tick, and Tom. I knew Horace. Where you went in to pay your bill at the water department, he was there behind the grill.

"Mother sort of took a disliking for Horace because he worked inside with his hat on. She saw no reason for that. Tom was the one I knew best in that family. Tick was in with a crowd of boys I went with, but a little older, and he later became an automobile salesman and then passed away.

"Tom was the youngest one. He was a clerk for either the Gulf Oil Company or an insurance firm in the Hurt Building.

"The place where all the boys hung out in that neighborhood of Tenth, Twelfth, and Thirteenth Streets was at Peachtree and Tenth, Marshall's Pharmacy . . . the drugstore cowboys, as we called them.

"And we'd meet up there every night to gossip, etc. Tom was there often. He was a very nice boy. I look back on him with pleasure. Reuben Donaldson, the son who lived on Twelfth Street, was called Rube, of course.

"Incidentally, there is a Sardis Methodist churchyard just off Roswell Road where there is a single mausoleum, the Donaldson family mausoleum. Old man Silas died, I think, about 1893 and was buried there, along with several others.

"The mausoleum has been allowed to deteriorate; the roof leaks, and the slate roof slid off. They hadn't repaired it, but I hope they now have. That was the crypt and burial place of the Donaldson family, though they are not all in it, by any means. In fact, Captain Tom is at Oakland. He was moved from Sardis to Oakland many years after he died in 1920.

"Then, on the other side of Thirteenth Street, beginning back of the Dunbar Roy home, was the Fair Dodd home. Fair Dodd was an insurance man. He had a son, Richard. Fair Dodd was the partner in Haas and Dodd. Dick Dodd was my contemporary, and in later life he moved to Montezuma, Georgia, where he had a large peach orchard. I think he's still living.

"And then the Meakin house next door, and the Hopkins house. Mr. Hopkins was an insurance man . . . R. J., I believe it was. He had a son, John Hopkins, who was about my age, maybe a year or two older.

"Next door was Dr. Perry. Dr. Perry was a medical doctor and every time one of the boys hurt himself, they'd call Dr. Perry. He was a great big man, rather ungainly . . . never would have made the track team . . . but he was a great asset to the neighborhood.

"And the Bratton family was next. They had two daughters, Annie and Martha. They were both very attractive, Martha especially. She married . . . the name doesn't come to me now. I don't think she's still living.

"Then for a stretch on the north side of Thirteenth Street were several shotgun houses. The lots dropped off in the rear, so in the front they were up level with the street. The folks lived there were good, honest people, not wealthy, of course. I remember particularly one family, the Bennett family. They had a son named Gordon Bennett, who was my contemporary. We liked each other very much. His father was in the dairy business. His name was Swan Bennett. He was very muscular. He could hold out his arm this way, and the smaller boys could chin on it. Of course, we marveled at the strength of Mr. Bennett. His wife was a very nice, affable lady. Gordon had a sister, Josephine. I think she's deceased now. I know Gordon is.

"Then the last house, there was a vacant lot, and then the duplex we lived in. Next door to us was a bungalow where a family named Thornton lived . . . Chancellor Thornton. I think there were three of those Thornton boys. The oldest one, Harden, was in the army in World War I. We all looked up to him because he was older and in uniform.

"Then there was a one-story house. I'm trying to remember the name of the family that lived there. Anyway, they had chickens in the back yard. In that day and time you could have chickens in your yard, or even a hog, if you wanted one. When we lived on Thirteenth Street, I was often awakened in the morning by the crowing of roosters, which wasn't an unpleasant sound. Billygoats? Seems to me somebody in the neighborhood had one.

"The last house on that side was the Slaughter home . . . W. Quinn Slaughter. They were a very genteel family. Mrs. Slaughter was a bit hard to get along with. She was always cussin' the boys out. She had no sons, had three daughters, Mary Lee—who married a lawyer and moved to Birmingham, Alabama—Sarah, and Jane.

"Sarah was a year or two my senior, but a very attractive blonde girl. She never married. She was librarian for an insurance company for a long time in Atlanta and a pillar of St. Mark's Methodist Church. Sarah died recently, another link to my childhood.

"The younger daughter, Jane, is still livin', I think.

"The Slaughter family moved from Thirteenth Street to the Prado . . . South Prado, to a two-story house where Sarah continued to live for the rest of her life. They must have moved from Thirteenth Street about 1916.

"I don't remember any community problems with children. Of course, there are always some weirdos in all neighborhoods. When it got dark, there was a streetlight near our house on Piedmont, and the boys would assemble there just to talk. We had sense enough to go in. Never had to call us. There were lots of front porches . . . some of them screened. We didn't use our porch so much . . . it went around the house, about half-way, facing a vacant lot, and we didn't use it much, I remember.

"My father was very friendly. My mother was one of a quiet disposition, a brunette. I remember asking my father one time if the barber charged him the full price for a haircut. His reply was that he sure did . . . he had a hard time finding any hair to cut. I don't remember his having any hair at all . . . got bald early.

"As I said, sitting on the front porch was a favorite custom because if there was any air circulating, you could get it sitting on the porch . . . long before air conditioning.

"The house directly across the street from us on Thirteenth Street is still there. It always reminded me of a steamboat in conformation, and about a year after we settled in on Thirteenth Street, the Douglass family came to live there. They had four children. I always thought of Mrs. Douglass as a very nice lady. She was born in LaGrange. Her father was Judge Tuggle, of one of the courts down there. She taught school at the Home Park School. That was something of a chore to get there when she was teaching. Her husband was one of the quietest men I ever knew. He liked to work with his hands. He was a night clerk for the Railway Express. He was a very reserved man. I don't know that I ever heard or saw him laugh. I was one of his pallbearers when he died.

"As I said, the Douglass family had four children. The oldest one, William O. Douglass, turned out to be a close friend of mine. He was born in 1902. He was a big boy, and I was a small boy. Bill liked to camp out and hunt and that sort of thing. I never became a hunter. I don't like to kill anything but bugs.

"William was sort of an outdoor man, and every now and then he would suggest that we camp out somewhere at night. I went on several camp-outs with him, having assured my mother that he was an older fellow and could take care of everything.

"William was educated as a civil engineer. He dropped out of Tech needing only about one more hour of instruction. I never understood why he did that. But he was a civil engineer by profession. He was quite a talker.

"Well, let me get through with the Douglasses. The only daughter was Sarah, a brunette. She was very attractive, and the first real date I ever had was with her. She is still living, the widow of Steffen Thomas.

"Although I would have thought that Steffen would have been a little difficult to live with, the marriage apparently worked all right. Steffen was a sculptor, of course, and he was his own worst enemy in selling his sculpture. If you didn't like it, he just told you you didn't have any taste. But I liked him anyway.

"Steffen Thomas had a stab at the Stone Mountain Memorial, but I don't think it ever got very far. So did Julian Harris. Actually, between you and me, I always liked Julian Harris's work better than Steffen's. Steffen was inclined to be a little *moderne*.

"That fountain at Fifteenth Street, where the metal part gives forth water, Steffen designed that. It was pretty good.

"Anyway, Sarah married him right at the beginning . . . or right in the middle of the Depression. When you're hard up, you aren't going to pay anybody to do sculpture. So Sarah taught school. She always had a good mind. I think she taught mathematics over at the Laura Haygood School on Howell Mill Road and Tenth Street.

"Sarah is still living on Mentell Drive in a house that Steffen built. When he built anything, he built for the ages . . . stonework, etc. Every now and then I call her up to see how she is. She is rather retiring.

"Then the third child was Albert. Albert was a very handsome youngster and young man, but he sort of got off on the wrong track.

"The youngest child was Warren. Warren has lived in South Georgia for years. I remember when he was born in 1918, right across the street from us. He was the fourth and last child of the Douglass family.

"Bill Douglass, my special friend, preferred living away from nearly everything. His first marriage produced two children, . . . but the marriage ended in divorce, I think. He never married again. He moved up to Ellijay, Gilmer County. He lived out of town. Then I think he moved to Blue Ridge, or at least out from Blue Ridge, and lived by himself. I remember I visited him, oh, two or three times a year. . . . Would spend the night at his home, and then come back to Atlanta. Bill is gone now and is buried in a cemetery out from Blue Ridge where he had lived. He'd have been a good pioneer. He seldom cursed. He was a boy of good habits. (Oh, I cussed some . . . like boys growin' up . . . had no talent . . . just occasionally got annoyed.)

"On the corner of Pause Street, Mr. Grizzard ran a grocery store there for many years.

"On the corner was the Lokey home. Dr. Hugh M. Lokey . . . let's see, Hugh, Jr., was his eldest son. Hugh, Jr., was with Firestone in Texas for a long time. I saw recently where his widow had died. Then came Boyce, who was better known to her friends as Pokey Lokey.

"Hamilton Lokey was the third child. Ham's still living, of course, so is Charlie, the fourth and youngest son. The two oldest ones are gone . . . Hugh and Boyce. Boyce was married to Harold Martin, who is also now gone. Boyce died several years ago.

"Oh, I forgot the Callaway family, who lived about halfway down the street. They had a son named Spencer and a daughter named Helena. Helena became my sister's best friend."

CHAPTER 5

Work at Western Union and Death of First Sweetheart

Franklin was eighteen years old, and his future was looming. Though not much was made of the decision at that time, Franklin then made a choice that would direct the rest of his life. He elected not to go to college but to educate himself through books and experience.

"I decided to seek my education in other directions," he recalls. "Georgia Tech would not have been my bag. I wasn't excited about higher mathematics. Had I gone to college directly from high school, I think it would have been the University of Georgia, or maybe Oglethorpe. I have always felt very close to Oglethorpe, and in 1970 they gave me a doctorate— Doctor of Humane Letters. I had to make a baccalaureate address for them that year also.

"Next door to us was the Worthen family—Herbert C. Worthen, who was a big shot with Western Union. He was the manager of the Southern Division of the Western Union Telegraph Company, and that was in a day and time when Western Union was very visible.

"They had messenger boys in uniform delivering telegrams in the neighborhoods, delivered by telephone to the business section unless they insisted on personal delivery.

"Mr. Worthen seemed to think I was a boy of some future and asked

Franklin M. Garrett, Western Union delivery clerk, ca. 1925. Photo courtesy of Franklin M. Garrett

me to come to work for him . . . which I did.

"At that time I sort of wanted to be a railroad man, but I got to the right age at the wrong time. I wanted to be in the operating department, not a clerk somewhere, and they were using heavy locomotives and longer trains. So I never got to be a railroad man.

"But I worked for Western Union for fourteen years. I didn't understand telegraphy. I wasn't in the operating department. I was in the delivery department. We were open the year around, every day of the year, so there were no holidays, and I was assigned my first job.

"I remember starting on July 4, 1924, as a delivery clerk in the Glenn Building. The main office was downtown on the corner of Marietta and Forsyth. Well, actually they were in the Journal Building, but the southeastern headquarters were in what was the Transportation Building, which later became the Western Union Building.

"So I was assigned to the Glenn Building as a delivery clerk. In other words, I had to see to it that all telegrams were sent out promptly by bicycle messenger. We had some walking messengers, too. We could walk all over town. So that's what I did there. People used Western Union messages for every kind of sentiment. And sometimes in my off hours I would make deliveries just for the fun of it. I never made deliveries in the part of town I knew so well. I'd go to any weirdo section. It didn't matter where. I had no fear of anybody attacking me at all, and nobody ever did. But I just did that for fun. I wasn't paid to do that. I enjoyed it, and then I was transferred to the general manager's office—Mr. Worthen's office.

"The man I was assigned to work for I will never forget . . . Thomas C. Alston. Mr. Alston was about my father's age . . . a short, bald-headed man, very affable. His father had been a telegraph operator before him. Tommy Alston. I was assigned to him, but the job was dealing with figures, and I wasn't too good at that.

"So after working in the general manager's office about a year, I guess, or maybe two (and I had made some good friends and contacts there), I was transferred back to the Atlanta city office . . . and for a good many years worked the early night shift. That was from four in the afternoon until midnight. The late night was from midnight until eight in the morning.

Glenn Building, 120 Marietta Street, 1952. Photo courtesy of the Atlanta History Center

Forsyth Street looking north at the Marietta Street intersection with the DeGives Opera House (center), 1917. Photo courtesy of the Atlanta History Center

"So I got some good experience working all sorts of hours and dealin' with people.

"My last job at Western Union was as branch manager of K.P., which was the designation for the office on Peachtree Street, at North Avenue, across from the North Avenue Presbyterian Church. Part of the Nations-Bank Plaza building now.

"Before I could qualify for that job, I had to go to Western Union school in Bloomfield, New Jersey, for about three months to learn how to operate those machines. I didn't have to operate them, but I had to know how.

"I boarded in a boardinghouse in Bloomfield. It was very close to the commuter line to New York City. . . . The line ran to Hoboken and crossed the river in a ferry, which was a whole lot more scenic than to go through a tunnel.

"Every opportunity I got I went to New York and just wandered around and looked the place over. They only paid me $50 a month the whole time I was up there, so obviously I couldn't be very extravagant, but that was a good experience, and when I finished in 1934, I came home on the train just in time to see my then sweetheart, the late Palmer Dallis, before she passed away.

"It was a terribly sad thing. It changed my life.

"I had begun dating Palmer in 1930. She was the daughter of Mr. and Mrs. Ernest E. Dallis. He ran the Dallis-Johnson Company. They were advertising agents. Palmer's mother was a Phelan, a very old Atlanta family, who incidentally built the Phelan apartments and Palmer apartments, which are now on the Historic Preservation list. Palmer's full name was Palmer Phelan Dallis. I met her when she was a bridesmaid at the marriage of Catherine Norcross to Son Richardson.

"Palmer was of short stature, very athletic, played on the various athletic teams at the Washington Seminary and the Junior League, and I was very much impressed with her. She was a brunette.

"I hadn't known her until the Norcross-Richardson wedding, but I managed to get an introduction, and we began to date. The Dallises lived at 3656 Peachtree Road, which is just beyond Peachtree and Roxboro Road on the left going out Peachtree.

"I didn't have a car then, but Palmer had a little two-seater automobile, and when we had to go anywhere on our dates, we used her car. I didn't have one until 1935. (It never occurred to me that my father would present me with one when I was sixteen, and it never occurred to him, either.)

"Incidentally, my father had only one car, as I remember. It was a 1924 Chrysler when they just started to make Chrysler. He didn't use it in his business especially, but we would take Sunday afternoon rides, and one very popular ride during the '20s was to ride out to Roswell and back. The road was paved, two lanes. That was a Sunday afternoon fun thing to do. I can't think why anyone would want to ride out to Roswell now, with all the traffic.

"My father was a very careful driver. He put on a cap, straight, clutched the steering wheel with both hands, and looked straight ahead. . . . He tended to his business driving the car. Mother never learned to drive, and I learned on that car.

"Back to Palmer. She had a combination of asthma and pneumonia, just before penicillin became available.

"She had just passed away when I got back from Bloomfield. Her aunt, McGowan Goldsmith, the wife of J. W. Goldsmith, took me upstairs where Palmer was laid out on a bed. That was the last time I saw her. It was a very hard, very sad time for me.

"I was one of the pallbearers at St. Luke's—one of the saddest days I have ever had. I think we would have had a good marriage. She had one sister, Epsie. Epsie married Harry Buice. Harry was with the Ivan Allen Company for a long time as a salesperson and went to Chicago in the same business. He finally retired, and they moved back to Atlanta. They are both deceased.

"I remember the pallbearers. I'm the only one still living. The others were Dr. Rufus Dorsey, better known as Dutch, Sid Hardy, Joe Cooper, Fritz Orr, and Green Warren. Green's brother Bill was a physician. Sam and Joe Cooper were architects. Joe was the junior partner. Joe Cooper married Tatty Howell. They are both gone now. They have a son named Harold Cooper. He is on the History Committee at the First Presbyterian Church. He is a rather tall fellow and has whiskers which flow like Santa Claus. Nice-looking man, tall like his father.

"I was manager of the K.P. office from 1935 until I voluntarily left Western Union, giving them plenty of notice, of course. I thought I would take a little time out to decide what I oughta do."

CHAPTER 6

1927

An Intrepid Bicycle Trip

Young Garrett may not have been an Olympic athlete as a youth, but he was known as a whiz on his bike. He moved like the wind on those wheels, showing up all over Atlanta and the surrounding near-by areas on his two-wheeler.

Thomas Hal Clarke, an Atlanta attorney, who was in the intermediate grades at Tenth Street School when Franklin was graduating, remembers when he came to school with an elastic guard around his legs to keep his pants from getting caught in the spokes. "He rode his bike everywhere," Clarke remembers.

Long after that, while he was in his early years with Western Union, Franklin set out on an astonishing solo marathon on his bicycle. It was a month before his twenty-first birthday, in August 1927. He was headed for Richmond, Virginia, and Baltimore, Maryland. Alone.

"I had talked it up with several other fellows, hoping they would ride with me, but they chickened out. I wanted particularly to see those cities because my father was born in Richmond and my mother was born in Washington, D.C., but had spent her girlhood in Baltimore. I had never seen either place."

This is the way he remembers it now. "I had a small knapsack and I think that is about all I took.

"The first night I made it to Anderson, South Carolina, using dirt roads, all heavily traveled. Anderson is 110 or 115 miles from Atlanta. I slept well that night, obviously. The next night I slept in Charlotte, North Carolina . . . then, let's see, the next night at South Boston, Virginia. I don't remember exactly what I spent, but hotels were cheap. A good hotel room with a bath was $2.50. My father traveled through the South, and he said he could always get good accommodations for about that price. I remember a hotel, Hampton Hotel on Houston Street, which was not a first-class hotel, but decent. They had a slogan, 'A room and a bath, for a dollar and a half.'

"I generally followed the main line of the Southern Railroad, going north, and passed through Gastonia, Charlotte, High Point, and Danville. (I departed from the Southern line because I wanted to go to a special restaurant.)

"The next night I spent at South Boston and then made it to Richmond. I stayed there only one day. Then I departed for Baltimore. I think that road was paved. The ride from Washington to Baltimore was the busiest segment of road I had traversed. At that time there were many fewer automobiles, and I didn't have to buck all those trucks. Freight went by rail then. I was traveling about one hundred miles a day. I had the wind behind me.

"I usually stopped for lunch or a hamburger. I didn't eat elegantly on that trip because I was not wearing a jacket, for one thing. Anyway, I spent a night or two in Baltimore.

"I remember when I checked into the hotel in Baltimore, I think they called it the Maryland, one of the bellboys wanted to know if I wanted a woman. I told him no.

"By that time my vacation was about to give out, and I didn't have time to ride back to Atlanta. So I caught the Piedmont Limited. I hadn't been on the train too long until it was lunchtime. As I said, I hadn't taken a jacket. I walked to the diner. I was neat, I guess. I had on a sport shirt, clean and all that.

"Each dining car had a steward. This one was dressed in striped pants and a morning coat, very dignified. When I walked into the diner and he looked me over, I said I needed lunch. He said: 'Young man, you will have to put on a jacket, we don't serve anybody without a coat.' I explained why I didn't have one. He had not heard that excuse before . . . so he considered the matter and finally said, 'Follow me. . . . He took me down to the end of the car, where they had a table with a curtain around it, and I had my lunch in solitary dignity.

"It was a fine trip, and I enjoyed it."

But it was apparently too tough for his friends to join him.

——— — ———

Atlanta had been impressed with the exploits of Bobby Walthour, an Atlanta man who had won the southern bicycling championship in 1896 and 1897 and was an inspiration to many young athletes. Walthour was often in the news as "King of the Cyclists" until his death at Boston City Hospital in 1949.

Writing of his exploits, newspapers had recounted that cycling had become popular in Atlanta by 1888, with clubrooms in the recently completed Y.M.C.A. at the corner of Auburn Avenue and Pryor Street.

Writing later in his book *Atlanta and Environs*, Garrett observed that by the mid-nineties, when bicycling had become a craze, women had joined for pleasure. Their riding costumes were carefully delineated . . . slightly above the ankle-length skirt, cut bell-shaped with organ pipe pleats at the back, short Eton jackets with big lapels, huge leg-o'-mutton sleeves, crinoline lined for cool weather. . . . High-buttoned or laced shoes and a sailor hat with a ribbon band completed the costume.

But members of the local ministry took a dim view of cycling for ladies. An exception, Dr. Henry McDonald, pastor of the Second Baptist Church, came to their rescue and declared that he hated to see innocent pleasure made into a sin, that he failed to see anything wrong or immoral in the mere riding of a wheel by ladies.

The bicycle etiquette of that day required that a gentleman meeting a lady at a wheel and stopping her for a chat stood and held the handlebars of her wheel.

In spite of all that, during the late 1890s bicycling became so popular all over the nation that Atlanta converted one of the 1895 Exposition buildings at Piedmont Park into one of the first indoor tracks in the South—the Coliseum. In his *Atlanta and Environs*, Franklin was to recall that "often the riders were whirling around parallel with the ceiling."

A marvelous sight to behold.

Bobby Walthour, Sr. (1878-1949), ca. 1920. Photo courtesy of the Atlanta History Center

*Garrett Acquires His First Directory and Joins
the New Atlanta Historical Society*

By the time he had been graduated from Tech High School, Garrett, an intense reader, had become convinced that the main advantage to study at great colleges and universities was the opportunity to learn from master scholars—the exposure to inspiring minds.

And always, since he had been a boy, he had been drawn to older men who had become his friends and mentors. He found their aspirations and achievements challenging, and they found him a surprisingly energetic young man who seemed to value the preservation of Atlanta's young and vivid history.

One of his favorite haunts was Miller's Book Store at 64 North Broad Street, which had been founded by John M. Miller in 1882. He came to the attention of Miller.

"After we got acquainted," Franklin recalls, "Mr. Miller said I could go upstairs and look around. Old used books had been stored on the second floor of the store. He said if I saw anything I wanted, I could just bring it down, and we would discuss it."

The first prize Franklin discovered was the *Atlanta City Directory* of 1886. It was to become the first in his treasured collection of Atlanta city directories.

Perusing that directory, young Garrett noticed that many lawyers listed in 1886 were still in practice in the early 1920s, or their law firms were still in existence then. He decided law firms were more apt to need and keep old directories than anybody else.

"Directories have a classified section, like the *Yellow Pages*," he explained. "So I began calling on some of the firms, cold."

Garrett's first acquaintance with the family of Margaret Mitchell, later author of *Gone with the Wind,* began in August 1927. Many law firms had offices in the Peters Building, and he noticed that the firm of Mitchell and Mitchell, composed of Eugene F. and Gordon Mitchell, had offices there. Eugene was Margaret Mitchell's father, and Gordon was her uncle.

"I knew of them, but I had never met them. This day I called on them without introduction.

"When I got into the reception room, I saw a bookcase which had some directories in it. I decided maybe I had hit the jackpot. A very nice middle-aged secretary, a Miss Bowen, came out and asked who I wanted to see. I told her my mission. She took me into the senior partner's office. He was, of course, Mr. Eugene Mitchell.

"I don't think I ever met a more scholarly man. 'Yes, young man,' he said. 'We have the directories back to when we began practice, but we use them. We do a lot of title research and land litigation, and we often have to find out where somebody lived in, say, 1881, and the directories will tell you that.

"'But you,' he told me, 'should be a member of the Atlanta Historical Society.'

"I hadn't heard a word about it. It had only been founded the year before, in 1926.

"Well, he got me in. And I now hold the oldest extant membership. And that's how I became acquainted with Mr. Eugene Mitchell, who was the vice president of the new Atlanta Historical Society.

"And that is how I got to know Walter McElreath, who was the founder and president of the Historical Society, as well as many older people I got to know.

"In those early days, the Society didn't have any headquarters. Whatever clerical work had to be done, like mailing out notices of meetings,

Dedication ceremonies, Father Thomas O'Reilly Memorial, Atlanta City Hall (left to right); Alex M. Hitz, Ella May Thornton, Robert R. Otis, Ruth Blair, Franklin M. Garrett, unidentified, Father Joseph R. Smith, October 1945. Photo courtesy of the Atlanta History Center

was performed by Miss Ruth Blair, whom I came to know and respect as a very capable person. She was one of the original members. She was then head of the Georgia State Archives and History.

"The meetings generally involved older people reminiscing, which, of course, I ate with a spoon. For years I was the youngest member, you know. I became acquainted with John Ashley Jones, who had been born in Atlanta in 1871. He liked to talk about Atlanta history, and I met other older men of the same caliber. So very early on as a very young man in his early twenties, I became acquainted with influential older men.

"They acted like they were glad to have me. They were always willing to associate with me and share information with me.

"As you know, I didn't go to college right out of high school, and I appreciated the company of learned gentlemen. I had already become a book collector before that time, of course.

"There were some other fine older folks, women—Miss Ella Thornton, Miss Blair, Mrs. S. W. McCauley, Mrs. P. Thornton Marye, and others.

"When I was twenty-six I became vice president of the Historical Soci-

Rhodes Memorial Hall (constructed 1903-1905), 1516 Peachtree Street, n.d. Photo courtesy of the Atlanta History Center

ety and a member of its Board of Curators. They call that the Board of Trustees now, so I hold the oldest membership in the Board of Trustees of the Atlanta Historical Society.

"For quite some time I served as secretary of the Society and kept the minutes. Then in 1942 I became president of the Historical Society. My term was interrupted when I had to go into the military for a period of time.

"The state of Georgia had just turned over the handsome Rhodes Building to the State Archives and History Department. The heirs of A. G. Rhodes had left that fine home to the state of Georgia, provided it would always be used for historic purposes. If they ceased to do that, it would go back to the Rhodes heirs, so the state has always been careful to see that it is used for historical purposes.

"We held meetings of the Atlanta Historical Society from time to time in the Rhodes Building. We also met in members' homes.

"Earlier, Lucian Lamar Knight, whom I never knew personally, had founded the Georgia Department of Archives and History, and Miss Ruth Blair was his protégé.

"One of the leading members was Mr. Walter McElreath. It was his ambition that we would have a home of our own. Mr. McElreath was a lawyer. He was closely associated with the Life Insurance Company of Georgia. The McEachern and Sheffield families, all important in the founding of the Life Insurance Company of Georgia, came from the same neighborhood over around Lost Mountain in Cobb County and Paulding County. That was Mr. McElreath's original home, too.

"When Life of Georgia was orig-

Walter McElreath (1867-1951), ca. 1940. Photo courtesy of the Atlanta History Center

inated in 1891, Mr. McElreath became their lawyer. He was paid mostly in Life of Georgia stock. He never sold any, thank the Lord for that.

"The first real headquarters the Historical Society had were at the Biltmore Hotel. The Biltmore was the finest hotel at that time.

"Mrs. William Candler, who had become Mrs. Hanson after William had been killed in an automobile wreck, said we could have a suite at a sort of nominal rental until a better tenant came along. Then she would give us notice, and we would have to move. I remember well when we moved there because it was when I became president of the Society on January 1, 1942.

"By that time Margaret Mitchell's book had come out, and it was a sensation. That was in 1936.

"The next year Mr. McElreath had decided to put the Historical Society on a firmer financial basis. He knew that no group like that can accumulate much just on membership, so he got several of his wealthy friends—Robert Woodruff, John W. Grant, J. J. Spalding, Bulow Camp-

Biltmore Hotel, 1950. Photo courtesy of the Atlanta History Center

bell—to agree to become annual members at $250 a year for five years. That afforded us enough money to move into the Biltmore.

"J. J. Spalding became president then, but he was in his late years and didn't live very much longer, perhaps a couple of years.

"Well, Mrs. Hanson found a tenant who could pay more, and we then moved to the Erlanger Theater. (That was about the time I got drafted, but more on that later.) Miss Blair liked the Erlanger idea. She was interested in photographs and had a fine collection of them. There was a window right on Peachtree . . . had a sign ATLANTA HISTORICAL SOCIETY in gold letters outlined in black, so anybody driving or walking by on Peachtree Street could see our display. It was good promotion.

"But Mr. McElreath was still determined that we were going to have a home of our own. In 1946, I think it was, when the Jones house became available . . . a handsome home designed by Neel Reid in 1922 and 1923 for Dr. and Mrs. Willis Jones. Mr. and Mrs. Jones had both passed away, and two of their sons were living in the home with their families.

"It was on the market for, I think, $60,000. We had a choice between it and the Mrs. Lena Swift Huntley home, which was right across from the Pershing Point apartments. But we liked the Jones home better. It was a beautiful piece of architecture. I think Mac (Mr. McElreath) made the down payment. It took only about a year or two to pay for it with Mr. McElreath's help.

"We were there from 1947 until we bought the Edward Inman property, where we are now.

"When we bought the Jones home, I was still a bachelor. The board thought somebody ought to be in the house at night, and they asked me if I would like to live there. I certainly would! It was the prettiest house I had ever lived in. It had a suite of rooms, a library and living room, an enclosed sleeping porch (where I did a lot of my work on *Atlanta and Environs* incidentally), then a nice-sized bedroom and two baths. I lived there until I got married the first time in 1952. We moved then to the Huntington Apartments across the street, but I kept my headquarters in the Jones house . . . didn't have room in my apartment.

"When we got the Jones house, we also got the maid who lived there.

There was a servant's house and a garage in the back, as well as a formal garden. So this fine maid stayed for us. I didn't take my meals at that house . . . and of course lunched at The Coca-Cola Company, where I worked.

"We outgrew the Jones home, and parking on Peachtree was a problem.

"Of course, the Jones home was not built for a historical society and neither was the Inmans' Swan House for that matter, but we subsequently bought the Inman property in the latter part of 1967 and moved out there. Our operations were in the Swan House on the lower floor, primarily.

"The Inmans had moved into that fine house in 1928. It had taken a couple of years to build it, and Mr. Inman lived three years to enjoy the beautiful house. He died of a heart attack in the living room, what we called the morning room, and that left Mrs. Inman, a young and attractive widow, who continued to live there.

"Some of our board did not approve of our buying it, but we negotiated with Mrs. Inman's son, Edward, who was living in the house, and during our negotiations, she suddenly passed away.

"So we had to complete our negotiations with Edward and the Trust Company of Georgia, which was the executor of the estate. We got that paid for in a hurry. So we don't owe anything on the land or the buildings.

"Meanwhile, the Atlanta Historical Society inherited all of Mr. Walter McElreath's fortune. He had died in 1951 at the age of eighty-four. We didn't come to it until 1965, but it amounted to some five or six million dollars. And for a local historical society, we had it made . . . at least we thought we had. But our ambitions grew, and we still have to raise money for different things. But that bequest made us the best-funded local historical society outside of New York or Chicago.

"Mr. McElreath had married a Miss Anderson from Powder Springs, a sweet lady who died of natural causes. I remember her well. Sometime after that I think Mr. McElreath became interested in Miss Blair, who was an attractive person, but she was not interested in getting married.

"He then married a retired schoolteacher of suitable age for him, and that marriage was very successful. Her name was Mildred Dickey. They traveled a good deal late in life, and in 1950, by the terms of his will, the Historical Society inherited his entire estate, but not until the death of his second wife and his two elderly sisters.

"We didn't inherit the bequest until his second wife died in 1965, and by the terms of the will, we inherited the whole estate."

Presentation ceremony at Georgia Governor's Mansion (left to right); Wilbur G. Kurtz, Sr., unidentified, David O. Selznick, Clark Gable, Gov. E. D. Rivers, December 1939. Photo courtesy of the Atlanta History Center

Wilbur C. Kurtz, Sr., and Ona Munson (Belle Watling in Gone with the Wind) *at a reception for the premiere of the motion picture, December 1939.* Photo courtesy of the Atlanta History Center

CHAPTER 8

1930s

A Foursome of Fateful Friends —
McElreath, Kurtz, DuBose, and Garrett

When the Garrett family was living on Penn Avenue and Sixth Street, Wilbur G. Kurtz, Sr., lived only two blocks away on the corner of Eighth Street.

Mr. Kurtz was an accomplished artist, much admired, with a deep interest in the Civil War and especially the Atlanta campaign. He had a small studio in the rear of his house where he painted and sketched his architectural renderings.

"I really got acquainted with Mr. Kurtz this way," Garrett says. "In the late '20s or early '30s, he was doing a series of articles, mainly about the Civil War period, which he knew most about. He was doing these articles for the *Atlanta Journal Magazine*. In the course of one article, he said that if anybody knew where Elmore Street was, please call him. He had run across the name and didn't know exactly where it was.

"Well, of course, I knew where it was. He was very appreciative and said, 'Come by and see me sometime.'

"It wasn't long after that that I went to see him. The Kurtz family lived in a red brick house. In the rear over his garage was his studio. He paint-

Wilbur G. Kurtz, Sr., Beverly M. DuBose, Jr., Franklin M. Garrett, and Beverly M. DuBose, Sr., on the steps of the Henry A. Alexander residence on Peachtree Road, current site of Phipps Plaza, 1942. Photo courtesy of the Atlanta History Center

ed pictures and did a great many architectural renderings. In fact, I have thirteen of his original water colors in my house now . . . great treasures. That began a long friendship. He was twenty-four years older than I was.

"Mr. Kurtz had a friend four years younger, Beverly DuBose, Sr., with whom he was bonded through their fascination with the Civil War. Mr. Kurtz and Mr. DuBose had established a custom of spending Saturday lunch together at the DuBose home and then riding around Atlanta looking for anything old and historical."

In April 1930, their invitation extended to young Garrett.

"We'd have lunch at Mr. DuBose's house with Mrs. DuBose, always a gracious hostess, and at least two well-trained servants, a butler, and a cook in attendance. Then we'd set out in the car, just riding and looking at things. There were artifacts and relics of all sorts to be found on every battlefield nearby, and in many rural homes where the memories of the great war would always be fresh.

Franklin M. Garrett (r) and Wilbur G. Kurtz, Sr., location unknown, 1933. Photo courtesy of the Atlanta History Center

Franklin M. Garrett (l) and unidentified, location unknown, 1933. Photo courtesy of the Atlanta History Center

"I was then with the Western Union, which was open all the time. I couldn't get off every Saturday.

"Anyway, that began a long-standing friendship with Mr. DuBose. Mr. and Mrs. DuBose had two children, Beverly M. DuBose, Jr., who I think was born in 1918, and his sister, Betty, who was born in 1922. When I started going to the DuBose home, Beverly, Jr., who was later to form a wonderful Civil War collection, was a boy of twelve. As time went on he began to go out with us. His father was really a book collector, and Beverly, Jr., was an artifacts collector. He was interested in whatever he could find that had to do with the Civil War.

"Early on, young Beverly acquired a mine detector. Many other collectors had them. They would go over a battlefield, and if there was some metal under it, the detector would make a noise, and they'd pick the object up.

"When he first started, he could go out to the Kennesaw Mountain battlefield beyond Marietta, but when that became a national park, that was verboten, so he had to quit that.

"But he continued searching. . . . Searched all over the Southeast and put together one of the finest collections ever assembled. All Civil War artifacts. He died in 1986, and his collection was willed to the Historical Society, which now has built a big building which will take that collection and many others.

——— — ———

"Beverly, Jr., was much like his father in many respects. Then, of course, he had a son, Beverly III, who is generally known as Bo. I think Bo is now fifty-two or fifty-three. He is the son of Beverly DuBose, Jr., and Frances Woodruff of Columbus, better known as Duffie. She is a widow now and lives in a home on Garraux Road where her two married children and families live nearby. So that began my long and valued friendship with Beverly DuBose, Sr., and Jr. and later the third.

"I have digressed. I was talking about my rides with Mr. Kurtz and the senior Mr. DuBose. We would be riding around on Saturday afternoon, and they would make comments on the Andrews Raid or the Atlanta campaign. I enjoyed being a third member of that group. . . . That continued from 1930 until Mr. DuBose's death in 1953 . . . twenty-three years.

"My interest is not only the Civil War but all of Atlanta's history, of course, but the Civil War was probably the most dramatic part of it . . . the most destructive too, I must say. I have always said that war is organized vandalism.

"Incidentally, Mr. Kurtz did not drive an automobile. The only time I was in an automobile with him was sometime before that. It was in a Studebaker. He put the Studebaker in the garage, and goodness knows how long it was left there.

"Anyway, Mr. DuBose would pick Mr. Kurtz up. And then I picked Mr. Kurtz up. So I would go out there on Saturdays and have lunch with Mr. and Mrs. DuBose. She was a very charming woman.

"Her maiden name was Lula Dean Jones. She had three brothers; all of them were well known in Atlanta. One was Harrison Jones, a senior vice president and chairman of the board of The Coca-Cola Company . . . Saunders Jones, who was a bachelor and was with a large steel firm in Chicago but frequently came to Atlanta. The youngest brother was Bolling Jones, who headed the Atlanta Stove Works . . . whose widow still lives at the corner of West Paces Ferry and Randall Mill Road."

Thomas Hal Clarke, who had known Franklin as an older boy when they were both at the Tenth Street School, became a member of Walter McElreath's law firm after he had finished the University of Georgia and its law school. He renewed his acquaintance with Garrett also. Clarke has since been a longtime member of the Historical Society's Board of Directors and has observed Garrett's contribution to Atlanta's history.

Mr. McElreath and Garrett became very close friends, and their common bond was history, Clarke remembered: "Franklin had really become Mr. Mac's understudy as a historian. He and Stephens Mitchell, Margaret Mitchell's older brother, Gordon Mitchell, his uncle, Mr. Henry Alexander, Mr. John Ashley Jones, and Beverly DuBose, Sr., really depended on Franklin to do the legwork getting the Historical Society started. Mr. Mac just loved him and used him, in the proper sense, to develop him along the lines he had an inclination for."

Clarke has long represented the Mitchell family's interests in legal matters. He recalls that both the senior Mitchells were especially interested in Garrett, considering him a stable person with the intelligence to carry the work of the Historical Society forward. The Mitchells themselves were deeply committed to Atlanta history. Their forebears came from Clayton County—near Atlanta, and Franklin fit right into the mode of what they thought a historian should be.

"It has long been obvious that they made a correct choice."

In the future, these four names were to become the major donors to the establishment of the Atlanta Historical Society: McElreath with his fortune, Kurtz with his valuable depictions of Civil War scenes, the DuBose family with its stunning Civil War collection—which is the crown jewel of the Historical Society's new History Center—and Garrett with his histories and collections.

CHAPTER 9

Garrett Begins His Necrology and
Attracts First News Notice

In his early manhood, Garrett had begun to collect everything he could find that had any bearing on Atlanta's past, including every published history of Atlanta, all the way back as far as he could discover anything. He had assembled a complete run of city directories, which are invaluable for research.

"That took a little doing. I don't think you could do it now. You couldn't find them. Then, in the late '20s or '30s, I began noticing that some records of Atlanta mentioned some individual and then sort of left him out on a limb without accounting for him.

"I had become aware of tombstone inscriptions when I walked through the historic Oakland Cemetery sometime in the late '20s. At that time older inscriptions really told you something about the deceased, when and where they were born, sometimes who they had married, and all sorts of information, so that is when I decided . . .

"I conceived the idea of endeavoring to account for every white male citizen twenty years of age and over who ever lived in Fulton or DeKalb Counties. These are my geographical boundaries. I chose both Fulton and DeKalb because DeKalb was the mother county of Fulton.

"I decided I would record all inscriptions on tombstones in every

Franklin M. Garrett, 1933.
Photos courtesy of the
Atlanta History Center

cemetery within a thirty-mile radius of downtown Atlanta. I had to cut it off somewhere, or I would be out in Montana recording cemeteries. The thirty-mile limit would include all of several counties and parts of several others.

"November 4, 1930—I was twenty-four years old—was the day I recorded the first two inscribed markers on the Northside Park Baptist churchyard, formerly the Mt. Zion Baptist Church, at 1887 Howell Mill Road. That is beyond where Howell crosses the freeway now (there wasn't any freeway then), and those two markers are still there, I am happy to say.

"I got quite a lot of information about that cemetery from the late Miss Sara Huff, who identified quite a few of the people who were buried there.

"Back in those days I didn't have an automobile. I got about on a bicycle. As a matter of fact, I didn't have a car for five years after I started that project, but I kept going. At that time I was working for Western Union Telegraph Company, and I had rather odd hours most of the time, 4:00 to 12:00, or 12:00 to 8:00, etc., so I had some time to get out at odd hours and on weekends, Sundays.

"My cemetery records, which now include large cemeteries, now occupy twenty-two volumes, large recording-journal size, all bound. The journals come from office supply houses, pages already ruled and just right for my information.

"It has been very interesting. I went to such distances as McDonough, Norcross, anywhere within a thirty-mile radius, and in 1935, after I got my first automobile, I began using it to get about.

"Even today, if I hear of a cemetery I missed (and the only ones I could have missed would have been family cemeteries way back in the woods), I will go out and record it. A couple of years ago I heard of one I had overlooked out in old Campbell County, at Red Oak. A gentleman called me who'd heard about my cemetery records and said, 'There's a little one here on my place.'

"I went out there. It didn't take very long. There was just one inscribed marker. It was a Williams family cemetery.

"So you see, even today, if I hear of one I missed, I will go out and record it.

"Big cemeteries like Oakland take a little time. Oakland took from April to September 1933. Westview took quite a bit of time, too. I recorded it in 1935 and '36. That is a very essential record if you are compiling a necrology of counties.

"I mentioned at first that I was acquiring information on white males. . . . To try to do it for black men would have been impossible before the Civil War, when all but a few, who were free, just went by their first name. Obituaries are scarce for them, and all in all it would take more time than I have had to give it, but I hope that some scholar will do it for the black people.

"I spent a lot of time in the DeKalb and Fulton County courthouses recording such information as marriages, wills, inventories, and appraisals of estates, all of which work into this necrology, and essential facts that I want to record about each person are on these forms.

"I have the forms printed ahead of time, and I will fill them out, one for each person. The essential information is the surname, three names if there are three, and the nickname by which he was known, if he had a nickname. I'll throw that in with quotation marks, exact date and place of birth, the date of his arrival here in case he wasn't born here, the names of his parents, including the maiden name of his mother, the names of his wives, if he was married more than once, his occupation, no matter what he did, whether he was a street sweeper or head of the biggest bank in town, whatever public office he might have held, anything from the justice of the peace on up. If he lived in the city, his residence address.

"Many people lived in one place fifty years, and others moved every time the rent came due. In that case I would use the last address, the date of death, the cause of death if other than natural (they may have gotten tired of life and jumped off the roof of the Candler Building, or been hit by a streetcar crossing the street, or maybe drank a bottle of carbolic acid, which would suggest an extreme disenchantment), the place of burial, so each person would be accounted for from birth to death.

"I don't go into any military details, but if he participated in the Revolutionary War, Mexican War, World War I, and in the case of the Civil

War, either Confederate or Union, because some of our citizens were in the Union Army.

"So that about wraps it up. Of course, a necrology wouldn't comprise a complete biography, but it is what you need for doing genealogical research.

"Genealogy is of interest to many people. We have people coming to the Historical Society every day doing genealogical research, and some of my records have been reproduced on film. I visualize my necrology being in book form, however, in alphabetical order. I started off this past fall putting the necrology together, and I am having a good time doing this in my spare time. I am now working on the year 1906. I had to start somewhere, and that's the year I was born.

"I am down to about November 20, and the pile of these forms is this . . . this high. When you go backward in time, the information is less voluminous, but as you come this way, the information is more voluminous. Eventually it will include the year 1821, when white settlers were first permitted to come in, through the year 1931. . . . I had to stop somewhere.

"In January 1932, two counties were added to Fulton. I didn't want to enlarge my geographical territory. The new ones were Campbell to the south, for which Fairburn had been the county seat, and Milton County to the north, of which Alpharetta was the county seat.

"So if a man passes away on December 1931, he is in, but if he holds over until 12:01, he's out. Of course, it could be picked up later and brought forward. There are no necrologies around with the scope of mine. Gwinnett County has done a pretty good job, but they don't give as much information as mine, like occupation, which is important to define a man.

"Newspaper obituaries are good sources. I've gone back through all the newspapers as far as they go, back to 1857 in this area. I visited Yale University in May of 1988. I had heard they had bound volumes of Atlanta newspapers older than we have here, and they did have a few. Newspaper accounts are very important outside of cemetery records, courthouse records, census records, etc. (I don't like to look through a machine.)

"I have had the census of DeKalb County for 1830, 1840, 1850, 1860, 1870, 1880, and 1900. The 1890 census was destroyed by fire in Washington, so that isn't available to anybody. It's gone. Another source has been interviews with older people. I've done a great deal of that. Most of them are gone now who would remember anything I need to know. Almost all the county histories are useful. I refer to those frequently.

"I have all city directories of Atlanta. A city directory will list a person and give the last name. If she is a widow, they will say who she is a widow of. A man's listing would be last name, first name, initial, his occupation, his address, where he lived, his wife's first name (following his in parentheses); some of the directories even list the people who died the year before . . . listing them alphabetically.

"The ads are fascinating in all directories. I don't think I could put together another set. The only one before the Civil War, 1859, has ads for slave dealers, well diggers, carriage builders, and occupations that are long gone. They are a very important source. They give the addresses and other facts I need for individuals. I try to spend some time each day working on this at home. I have probably the most complete private library on Atlanta's history anywhere around.

"I run into some variations between obits, cemetery records, and others, and if I must choose one, I choose the cemetery. But I've found some that weren't accurate. There is one on top of Vinings Mountain in the old Pace Cemetery. . . . White gentleman, Mr. S. S. Yarbrough . . . the tombstone had him passing away in 1916, and he actually died in 1915. . . . I had abstracted his obituary from the newspaper. If your obit is in the newspaper at a certain time, chances are you're dead then. So the volume of information I have is very large.

"These people became personalities to me. . . . Sometimes there will be photographs of obscure people who've died in the poorhouse, in jail, because they were citizens one time or another. The rich are easier to identify. So the rich and poor, the young and old, all are candidates for my necrology. They must all be twenty-one. They must have lived in the county long enough not to be considered transients. Many of them simply moved away and disappeared. . . .

"I worked for sixty years acquiring all of this information . . . abstracting newspaper obituaries, cemetery records, inscriptions, courthouse records, wills, inventories, and appraisements of estates, death certificates, all sorts of biographical information about people. . . . Young or old, rich or poor, it didn't matter. They have lived. . . . That is what has counted with me."

———   —   ———

First Newspaper Acknowledgments

As early as 1930, young Garrett was attracting attention for his historical collections. In the *Atlanta Journal* that summer, William O. Key, Jr., wrote:

> But in Atlanta is a young man who seems to have directed his most unusual talent for collecting in what is all probability one of the most useful channels, and at the same time is perfecting his accumulations to a more definite completion than one could suppose possible, considering the short length of time he has practiced his avocation.
>
> "He is Franklin M. Garrett, son of Mr. and Mrs. Clarence R. Garrett of 811 Penn Avenue, N.E. Mr. Garrett, who is only twenty-four years of age, has been following the lure of his hobby for more than eight years. Today he has the only known private collection of every city directory ever published in Atlanta and . . . other collections, too . . . but it is the unremitting effort spent in his search for them that lends distinction to this young man's attainments.
>
> "He has declared that his purpose is to publish the names of all dead who were regular citizens of Atlanta, and not to exclude the socially low or financially humble. 'It certainly limits the field of history to include only those persons who were influential or affluential,' he says. 'My idea is to include every person possible and to tell everything about him that is available.'

Key commented on Garrett's study, apparently in his parents' home:

> It is a cheerful little room with bookcases lining the walls, each volume in perfect order, dustless, clean and tidy. There are many tomes of biography and history, a defiant Spanish galleon in miniature on a small bookcase, sails billowing, two models of American locomotives, two early American samplers, an ancient map on the wall here and there and back of it all, row on row of the mute history of Atlanta, with the thousands of men and women who have lived and died, thousands lost trace of, forgotten in forgotten places.

Key continued: "One may ask, 'Who was he?' 'What did this one do?' Or, 'Where did she live?' and while people may not remember, the old directories of Atlanta remain alone to tell the story."

Key's laudatory article covered almost a full page in the newspaper.

——— — ———

About the same time, in July 1930, Atlanta was hysterically proud of another native son, Robert Tyre (Bobby) Jones, Jr., who had just won the grand slam of golf, a feat never before accomplished. He arrived back in America from his British conquests aboard the *Europa* on July 2, 1930, to a tumultuous New York welcome, including the bellowing of whistles and an aquatechnical display from lifeboats.

Wrote Ed Danforth in the *Atlanta Journal:*

> Bobby Jones rode through hero's canyon at mid-afternoon along the trail where New York has thundered a nation's greeting to Pershing, Lindbergh, Ederle, Chamberlin, Byrd and Kingsford-Smith and today the city roared a welcome no less significant in spontaneity and spectacular qualities.
>
> "The bronzed hero who rode through the vast gulch in the financial district of New York was wearing the chaplet of peaceful conquest. His cannon were wooden driving clubs, his shrapnel was a tiny rubber ball, his airplane was a steep

pitch to a patch of green. The channel he had crossed was the Atlantic Ocean where he had discovered the vulnerability of the British Amateur and open golf trophies and had brought them back home.

In Garrett's *Atlanta and Environs*, published twenty-four years later, the entire celebration for Bobby Jones covered ten pages, including the memorable line from the caddies at the Capital City Club: "Welcome home, Mr. Bob. You sho' brought home the bacon."

Robert Tyre (Bobby) Jones, Jr. (1902-1971), ca. 1926. Photo courtesy of the Atlanta History Center

CHAPTER 10

Real Estate, Law Degree, and Coca-Cola

"As I said, I was thinking about what I should do. . . .

"Another neighbor on Penn Avenue was E. A. Erwin, Bo Erwin, everybody called him. He was with Draper-Owens Company and knew more about business property on Whitehall Street than anybody I ever knew, because much of his business was from leasing. In the real estate business you make a lease, and you get a certain percent from the rental every year . . . steady income as opposed to sales commissions.

"The early part of 1939, January 1, or along then, I was just thinking. I was living at home, paying my parents a small amount of rent, of course, so I figured that real estate, with my knowledge of Atlanta, would be a good deal for me.

"Mr. Erwin took an interest in me and told me to see Ward Wight and Company. Mr. Wight's office was in the Healey Building, so I went down and talked to him.

"I was employed by him as a salesman for Ward Wight and Company. He turned out to be a very fine boss.

"He had working for him the late Cone Maddox, Sr., and the late Stewart C. Bird, who married a daughter of Samuel C. Dobbs, one of the big wheels in the early history of Coca-Cola. I got along fine with these people and started a real estate career. I began to specialize in the sale of apartment buildings. At that time Asa G. Candler, Jr., better known as Bud, was buying apartments. Bud Candler was never associated with The Coca-Cola Company, but he was interested in his family's real estate holdings.

"Bud was said to be a little difficult to get along with, and some people said for me not to go see him . . . but I didn't take any stock in that. My dealings with him were very pleasant.

"When I was with Ward Wight, the Woodrow Wilson College of Law was right next door. It was run by ex-governor Clifford Walker and Dean Kilbride. I had been fascinated by legal terms . . . then as now I did a lot of reading . . . so I decided the way to learn legal terms would be to study law. So I took a two-year course. It was at night, and I didn't have far to go to get there. I enjoyed it very much.

"I have always wanted to give everybody his just dues, so I made my best grades in equity. I made my lowest grades in practice and proceedings because I didn't have the intention of practicing law anyway.

Franklin M. Garrett, dressed as Atlanta pioneer Hardy Ivy, appears at an Atlanta pageant with Mrs. E. Y. Howard (l) and Mrs. John Spalding (r), November 1938.
Photo courtesy of the Atlanta History Center

But law itself had always interested me.

"I have here the first of 112 volumes of the Georgia Supreme Court Reports. I collected those years ago. They extend from 1844 to 1900. I've read every case that went to the court from DeKalb or Fulton County. There's a whole lot of history in those. That's another thing I did which helped me in developing my necrology.

"One of the most interesting cases is in the Forty-eighth Georgia. I believe it was in 1879 . . . when the first pastor of the Rock Springs Presbyterian Church . . . the one over on Piedmont at Montgomery Ferry, was a young man. His name was Myron D. Woods. He was charged with the seduction of Miss Emma Shivers, who was the daughter of the poet Thomas Holly Shivers, the friend and contemporary of Edgar Allan Poe.

"In that case they put all the evidence in the court report, making it rather a racy report. I think he was convicted, but was just left in his post without any more problem.

"Many other cases were interesting, but few had any sex, of course."

With a new LL.B. after his name, Garrett had built up a modest income from leasing and real estate sales commissions and had no thoughts of leaving Ward Wight's real estate firm.

——— — ———

Three years earlier, on Gen. Robert E. Lee's birthday, January 13, 1937, Garrett had become a member of the Piedmont Driving Club. He was sitting on the club's terrace on a Sunday afternoon when he received an invitation few young Atlantans have ever refused. He was asked to interview at The Coca-Cola Company.

——— — ———

Driving Club Minutes

The Piedmont Driving Club was organized in the spring of 1887 as a gentlemen's association where wives and children of members might be taken without fear of meeting with improper characters. No gamblers or shysters would be permitted to become members.

There was some disagreement about the possible location. With a little mischief in his mind, Garrett, who had become a member of the Driving Club in 1937, took pleasure in his book *Atlanta and Environs* in recounting the minutes of a preliminary Driving Club meeting as reported in the *Constitution* on April 15, 1887:

"Mr. Joel Hurt asked Mr. Hoke Smith if the same powers could not be exercised over a park in DeKalb as could be exercised over a park in Fulton.

"Mr. Smith said, 'No.'

"Mr Hurt said Mr. Smith's opinion was contrary to the opinion of nine-tenths of the lawyers in Atlanta.

"Mr. Smith said he was sorry for nine-tenths of the lawyers in Atlanta.

"Mr. Hurt said he was sorry for Mr. Smith.

"Mr. Smith said Mr. Hurt need not agitate his feelings about what Mr. Smith might know or not know about law.

"Mr. Smith said that if the park could be located separately . . . in DeKalb, it would stop the kickers.

"Mr. Phelan thought Mr. Smith and his friends were the kickers.

"Mr. Kiser wanted to vote.

"At that point, a great uproar occurred, owing to the fact that from six to a dozen persons wanted to express their views at the same time.

"Various and sundry motions were made . . . even President Kingsbery, who was on the ground, so to speak, gave evidence of being considerably dazed.

"Mr. Kiser thought all those present, except Mr. Smith, could vote then and that Mr. Smith could vote Monday night.

"There was some uproar.

"Mr. Rice tried to speak.

"So did everybody else.

"Mr. Rice was heard to say that he didn't propose to be drowned out. He would stay until morning but that he would be heard.

"Judge Newman tried to pour oil on the troubled waters.

"Thereupon every man who could get anyone to listen to him made a speech, discussing everything from sewer branches to the Piedmont Exposition.

"There were loud cries of 'call the roll.'

The meeting proceeded amid much uproar.

"'Let's leave the room!' shouted a voice.

"'Don't be foolish!' shouted another.

"'I wish you, . . .' exclaimed Mr. Kiser, but no one ever found out what it was he wished.

"Mr. Don Bain stood on a chair and shouted, 'I want to say one word!'

"'There's no quorum here!' shouted someone. 'There ain't thirty paid members in the house . . .'

Mr. Smith spoke on the quorum question.

"To keep down a riot Mr. Inman refrained from voting the proxy.

"When Mr. I. P. Inman's name was called, he asked Mr. Hoke Smith if he might vote. Mr. Smith told him he could, so he voted."

Mr. Smith declined to vote.

Mr. Phelan asked him to please vote, but he wouldn't.

There were thirty-three votes, ten nays and twenty-three yeas. That was not a quorum. There was another uproar. The assembled citizens put on their hats and walked out.

Five days later, on April 19, after the dust had settled, the Driving Park Association met again. Harmony prevailed this time. It was unanimously voted, after Mr. Walker agreed to sell his home, to buy the Walker tract, comprising 189.43 acres lying in land lots 54, 55, and 106 of the Seventeenth District of Fulton County. On July 1, 1887, a warranty deed for the consideration of $38,000 was made by Benjamin F. Walker to the Gentlemen's Driving Club.

In commenting upon the meeting of April 19, the *Constitution* reported:

"The meeting was from first to last harmonious. Everybody seemed to be in good humor and enthusiastic over the result."

——— — ———

Garrett's invitation to interview at Coca-Cola came in a somewhat jocular manner. His knack for remembering names, places, and dates came into play.

"I became aware of two men walking in my direction. One of them

Franklin M. Garrett, spokesman for Coca-Cola, 1943. Photo courtesy of the Atlanta History Center

was DeSales Harrison, who at that time was vice president and assistant to the president of The Coca-Cola Company, one of the highest offices in the company.

"DeSales had already become aware of my ability to remember names and dates. He saw me sitting there. He was with his father-in-law, Robert B. Pegram. He walked over and said, 'Franklin, I want you to meet my father-in-law, Robert B. Pegram. Incidentally, when did Mr. Pegram become a member of the Driving Club?'

"It so happened that I had been looking over the roster and had noticed that Mr. Pegram had become a member in 1920. I answered, 'I believe, Dee, that it was 1920.'

"Mr. Pegram was surprised. They were both surprised. When DeSales ran into me after that, he would always ask, 'When did this man come to Atlanta, when was he born?' challenging me, so to speak.

"So Harrison invited me to come over to the company, and he introduced me to Delony Sledge, Price Gilbert, and Arthur Acklin. Mr. Acklin was president of the company at that time. I didn't know much about Mr. Acklin, but I knew he came from Carroll County. He used to say, 'I was born on Buck Creek in Carroll County.'

"The interview went nicely. I was invited to join the company. I already knew The Coca-Cola Company was always a good place to work. That was in 1939.

"We agreed ahead of time that I wouldn't be transferred all over the world, that Atlanta was my beat. That was fine because they sort of wanted me to put the history of the company together. That had to be done at the home office, so I was assigned to Price Gilbert, an Atlanta bachelor who was soft-spoken and very bright.

"He was also the most diffident boss I ever had, never making any demands. He would stroll past my desk and say, 'Now, Garrett, what are you workin' on today? Maybe we ought to do this. . . .'

"One day he came by, leaned on the door, and said, 'Mr. Garrett, everybody here, except the men who work in the syrup plant, are supposed to be able to get up and make a few remarks on short notice . . . make a talk.' He said, 'I will tell you how to do it. You stand up and say, "Ladies and Gentlemen, where I now stand was once a va-a-a-a-a-st wilderness."

Nobody can say that wasn't so, so you may get a little round of applause. Then, if you can't think of anything else to say, you can continue as follows, "Wild animals once roamed, to and fro, . . . " and if you can't think of anything else to say . . . just sit down.'"

Garrett laughed heartily at this memory. He had been expressing his thoughts to his elders and betters for years.

Garrett had kept busy with the Atlanta Historical Society. In July 1942, the Society paid tribute to sixty-six living Atlantans, descendants of the 120 settlers who had been living here one hundred years earlier when the town changed its name from Marthasville to Atlanta. Brandishing the cane used by Marthasville's first town marshal, Garrett had introduced the speakers: Mayor William B. Hartsfield, Judge John D. Humphries, Dr. Glenn W. Rainey of Georgia Tech, President Goodrich C. White of Emory University, and Dr. Major F. Fowler, president of the Fulton County Medical Society. Garrett's Historical Society colleague, Ruth Blair, rang the city's oldest school bell to summon the guests to dinner at the Biltmore Hotel.

Then there was World War II.

"We all had to register for the draft in October 1940. I registered at Tenth Street School. The chairman of my draft board was Ralph McGill. As time went on, I began to wonder when they were going to get to me . . . so I called Ralph, whom I knew pleasantly. He said, 'We're not going to take you. We're not going to take anybody over twenty-six unless we get in the war. But if we get in the war, we'll take everybody!' So we got in with the Japanese attack on Pearl Harbor in December 1941, and they finally got to me in July of 1942.

"DeSales Harrison went into the navy. Price Gilbert went into the navy. The male force of the office was pretty decimated. I was in good health. The government was drafting young men from eighteen to twenty-six. I wouldn't have felt right not being in it. It wasn't just a 'boy' war. In 1943 they cut the maximum age from forty-six down to thirty-eight.

"I went into the service with a resolve of doing what they told me to do. I didn't ask for anything or say I didn't want anything. I was inducted at Fort McPherson in the classification section. Several of my friends were already in that section, and they wanted me there. So I stopped there, and that was my base the whole time I was in the army.

"It was a very interesting assignment. We had to interview and classify inductees from three states: Georgia, Florida, and Alabama. All the black inductees were processed at Fort Benning. That was where my good friend Delony Sledge was.

"My job was to interview each inductee very carefully and find out what his jobs had been, what his hobbies were, to see if he had some particular talent that would fit a particular place in the service. We had to interview everybody from illiterates to Ph.D.s, a very interesting job. One reason I was stopped at Fort Mac was my age.

"We had to give tests, sort of an intelligence test and an aptitude test. My good friend Tom Law made the highest grade in the aptitude test of anybody I interviewed. He was six years younger than I, and he did a good job classifying me.

"I remember one good old country boy. I had to ask him the names of his parents. His answer to that was, 'Well, they're dead.'

"I said, 'I'm sorry about that, but we've still got to have their names.'

"Many of the young men didn't have any particular skill, but a whole lot of them wanted to get into the air corps . . . that was sort of glamorous. We assigned as many as we could to what they wanted.

"I started as a buck private at $50 a month. Actually, the only sacrifice I made was the loss of income. That was mild compared with the sacrifices others made. At that time, I was living at 908 Juniper Street, in the Bon Air Apartments, which is still there. It was owned by Billy and Stella Wellborn, who also lived in the buildings. I was living there by myself, and the first week or two we had to stay at the fort in a barracks building, but as time went on, those of us who lived in Atlanta not too far away were allowed to live at home. I was still able to occupy my apartment.

"I had to get out to Fort Mac very early. We had to stand reveille, which is called before light in the morning, but we were soon relieved of that. It wasn't accomplishing anything for us. The two men I associated with were Bob Wood and Tom Law.

"We couldn't get out, any of us, until after the war ended. Germany surrendered first, but that didn't get us out. We had to wait until Japan

surrendered. We were eligible to get out. We had to pass a physical exam-
ination, but that was it. I remember that the doctor who examined me
was Dr. William B. Armstrong of Atlanta, a great tennis player at the Driving Club. I was in good shape and got out and went back home and
back to The Coca-Cola Company.

"Then I turned my hobby into a new job.

"I was assigned to the advertising department to assemble the company's history in some sort of order. Nobody had that responsibility. I
worked closely with Hunter Bell, a man I had always admired. Bell was
formerly city editor of the *Atlanta Journal.*

"One of my other duties was to answer letters from the public offer-
ing submissions for ideas for advertising, for which they hoped to get fees
. . . so I had to write those letters back to them. Sometimes they submitted
ideas we had used back in 1922. The easy answer was to point that out.
But I had to be careful not to obligate the company in any way legally.
In order to do that, I had to pass those letters to the legal department—
Joe Collins, Frank Troutman, and Julius Lunsford. Julius finally left
Coca-Cola to get into the trademark legal world. I think he retired early.
I worked closely with him.

"Frequently I had to be a witness in federal court when The Coca-Cola
Company sued a restaurant where they had served Pepsi or some other
cola drink when they didn't tell the customer what it was . . . or said it
was Coca-Cola. It was perfectly legal for them to serve Pepsi when they
told the customer, 'We don't have Coca-Cola, but we have Pepsi.' But
just substituting without telling was not legal.

"In those days, the idea was not to get money out of the fellow who
was doing the substituting, just to keep him from doing it without admit-
ting it. I had to appear in federal court and show how much money the
company had spent in advertising since 1886, and how many gallons of
Coke had been sold since then. Of course, that involved trips across the
United States. My job was not a traveling one at all, but I had to make
just enough trips to make it interesting.

"I had to attend some conventions. I remember a big one in 1948. The
Southern Railroad ran a special, the Crescent Limited, just to carry all
of us from Atlanta to Atlantic City. That was very interesting work. I also

had to make some presentations to bottlers at meetings, and to new employees just to tell them about the company.

"I want to make this one point. . . . My trips for Coca-Cola were practically all made by train . . . my favorite mode of transportation. They expected us to go first class. I never felt that I had to fly everywhere. The time spent on trains was my own time . . . so the traveling I did for Coke . . . I enjoyed all of it."

Garrett's Coca-Cola experience was more than mere enjoyment. It was the first time in his working career, indeed in his mature life, that he found himself associated with an organization focused on the future. His early employment had been rooted in the past except for his years with Western Union—an intriguing but unalterable past, to be understood and valued but not to be changed.

For Coke, the sky was the limit, and by the time Garrett had spent twenty-eight years with the company, Coca-Cola had become a multinational company with a clear command in the markets of the soft drink industry.

Garrett's early mentors had been his father's age, well situated and established, with enough leisure to turn their cultural attention backward. Now he worked with men and women, some older and many younger ones, whose outlook was open and engaged, busy and portentous.

Robert W. Woodruff, Coke's chairman and creative eminence, was at his peak as instigator and leader of innovations and improvements wherever he saw the need. To this end he utilized the talents of his own crew, carefully selected for their initiatives, as well as the potentials of his friends and colleagues in his community and the world.

Woodruff was Atlanta's premier capitalist-philanthropist, and remained so until his death in 1985 at ninety-five. As long as he was active, he worked behind the scenes as a vortex of ideas, a high-voltage human centrifuge spinning possibilities for his company and his region.

Among other duties, Garrett was assigned to gather and preserve the chronology of The Coca-Cola Company, which had begun in Atlanta in 1886. As company archivist, he was expected to organize and tabulate the development of its corporate structure, its leadership, its sales methods and plans, and its advertising, which was notable for its brilliance and effectiveness. It was an entirely new world to him, both stimulating and surprising.

Four years after he took early retirement from Coke to head the Atlanta Historical Society (for his second time as president), he was asked to put Coke's history in book form. The book was published in 1974 as *The Coca-Cola Company—An Illustrated Profile*, but his name was not on it.

"They seem to have a penchant for publishing without using the author's name. But I got a fee out of it, and it really didn't matter. It sold at bookstores and was distributed around to the businesses of Atlanta, firms who did business with Coca-Cola."

Garrett, as usual, remembered a "pleasant" association with the dynamic Woodruff.

"I never got invited down to Ichuaway, which suited me alright, since neither gin rummy nor hunting would interest me at all. Woodruff was not a talkative man. . . . He was handsome, very tall, and a born salesman.

"He was a firm believer in the accumulation of Coca-Cola stock. Somebody asked him one day, 'What was the price of the stock when you began selling it?' His answer was 'I never sold any.'

"He became president of The Coca-Cola Company in 1923, when he was thirty-three. If you're going with a company and can start off as president, that's not bad."

"One day he called me, didn't say who was calling. He just asked, 'Where's the Fall Line in Georgia?' I recognized his voice. The Fall Line . . . if you draw a line between Augusta and Columbus, that's the Fall Line. I gave that information to his secretary.

"Another time he called and said he and a couple of friends had organized what is now the Peachtree Golf Club. . . . He and John O. Chiles, Bobby Jones, and some others had played at the Capital City Club for a long time, but that got crowded and they had to wait to tee off, which didn't suit them at all.

"So they decided to organize a new club, and they didn't know what to call it. He asked for a suggestion. I had one. That club is in the Cross Keys district of DeKalb County. I submitted that name to him . . . the Cross Keys Club. But there was a restaurant downtown called by that name, and Mr. Woodruff and his friends were afraid people would get the restaurant and the club mixed up. So they set on a name by which nobody has ever gone wrong in Atlanta. They called it the Peachtree Golf Club. I was later asked to write a history of that club, which I did."

Mr. Woodruff was a great one for quietly doing things to help deserving people.

"One day I got a call from him that I was to be expected to be at his home on Thanksgiving morning. The call came the day before Thanksgiving. Nobody who got that call ever declined. So I went out, and there were several other men there, close friends of Mr. Woodruff's.

"He had conceived the idea that he must do something for Athos Menaboni, one of Atlanta's celebrated artists, who painted naturalist subjects. Mr. Woodruff had decided that every school in Georgia must get a life-size copy of the Georgia state bird and flower, painted by Menaboni, and he didn't want anybody to know he was responsible for it.

"He said, 'Do you think the Atlanta Historical Society would be willing to do that? . . . We were still at the Jones home at that time. I think it was about 1960. I assured him the Society would be happy to undertake this.

"The distribution was another thing. I went to see M. D. Collins, then superintendent of schools, to find out if they would assume the job of distribution. Dr. Collins was very happy to do it.

"That was an example of Mr. Woodruff's way of working anonymously . . . of getting something to the children of the state, also a way of getting Mr. Menaboni's work distributed and better recognition for his talent. Mr. Woodruff was very generous to people, honoring their work."

Garrett's friendships with younger associates began in his early days at Coke when so many of the men were called into military service.

Thomas C. Law, Jr., one of his colleagues, some years younger, recalls that he and some of his buddies had a regular get-together at which the price of admission was a story, or a joke.

Franklin allowed he was fresh out of funny stories, but he would sing a song. He did so, rendering two stanzas of "The Wabash Cannon Ball" in a ringing baritone voice.

From the calm Pacific waters,
To the rough Atlantic shore,
Ever climbing hills and mountains,
Like no other did before.
She's as graceful as a comet
Smoother than a waterfall
It's the Western Combination
It's the Wabash Cannon Ball.

There is music in her jingle,
There is music in her roar,
Like a will-o' wisp she travels
On her way from shore to shore,
May her greatness last forever,
May the glory never fail,
Of the Western Combination
Of the Wabash Cannon Ball.

Law, who retired several years ago as vice president in charge of U.S. soft drink sales for Coca-Cola, made this remark about Garrett: "When most of us are forgotten, Franklin will be remembered. He is a rare coin, the die is lost. . . . Hs dedication to his avocation was so comprehensive that it became his vocation."

——— — ———

Another former associate, Nathaniel C. Harrison, Jr., who retired from the executive staff of the office of the president of Coca-Cola, remembers Garrett affectionately: "What a marvelous gentleman! I first met Franklin when I joined the advertising department of The Coca-Cola Company in July 1948. He was in charge of archives—the history of the company, and any important happening through the years.

"He was more than that. . . . He was the superb source of all kinds of information: the town of Marthasville, Terminus, and Atlanta, but especially his knowledge of railroads. He knew every engineer and fireman on every train that ever ran. Maybe Casey Jones, whom he sang about while playing his harmonica. We will remember his limerick of J. B. King . . . from flatcars low, to boxcars tall . . .

"He has a great sense of humor and would entertain all of us with jokes from time to time, but especially when he would give his speech about the pitfalls of marriage to a would-be blushing bride.

"Franklin is one of a kind and a great friend."

Harrison, a talented musician who played first trumpet and was soloist for the "Sorta Forties" dance band for years in Atlanta as a hobby, composed a song for The Coca-Cola Company's choral club to sing for Franklin—to the tune of "Casey Jones":

(1)

Now Franklin Garrett is a railroad fan
He looks out the window every time that he can,
He knows every schedule and each engineer's name
As a locomotive watcher, boys, he won his fame!
CHORUS:
Franklin G., loves to watch the engines,
Franklin G., loves to watch the train,
Franklin G., loves to watch the engines
At a fifth-floor window, boys, he won his fame.

(2)

Now Frank hates diesels and electrics, too
To the old steam boilers he is always true,
He lets all the lovely women pass him by
But a six-eight wheeler is the apple of his eye.
CHORUS:
Franklin G., loves the old steam engines,
Franklin G., lets the ladies pass him by,
Franklin G., loves the old steam engines
A six-eight wheeler is the apple of his eye.

(3)

When Franklin is loungin' on his country estate,
And can't hear the moanin' of the evening freight,
He can blow this whistle with a mighty blast,
And make believe a choo-choo train is going past.

CHORUS:
Franklin G., can blow this little whistle,
Franklin G., can blow a mighty blast,
Franklin G., can blow this little whistle,
And make believe the evening freight is going past.

CHAPTER 11

Atlanta and Environs—
A Chronicle of Its People and Events
Is Published

In 1949, four years after the dramatic end of World War II, the Lewis Historical Publishing Company of New York had decided that Atlanta deserved a comprehensive record of its significant history. It sought a competent local writer to undertake the task.

Newspapers of the region boasted many accomplished writers, and the faculties of high schools and universities in the area were staffed with qualified academic teachers and professors of history.

But when the New York publisher approached the leaders of the Atlanta Historical Society, the elders found one man they thought would do the best job. Though he had only a few published historical essays to his credit, in addition to his business assignment of keeping the corporate records of The Coca-Cola Company, they nominated Franklin Garrett to undertake the challenging job. They knew he had spent his whole lifetime preparing for such an effort.

"I wasn't sure I could find the time," Garrett recalls. "No one had done anything resembling a complete history since 1902, really. Of course, I had already accumulated so much information. The Lewis people didn't make any rules, or give me a set deadline. So the burden was on me, and I had to put up or shut up. I went to work."

The world was changing fast. Mussolini had been killed by partisans in a grisly coup. Hitler had died in a Berlin bunker. The first atomic bombs had been exploded over Hiroshima and Nagasaki. Eighteen Nazi leaders had been sentenced to death by the Nuremberg Tribunal.

Harry Truman had been reelected president. The Truman doctrine had been announced, and Gen. George Marshall had called for a European recovery program in a speech at Harvard.

The first United Nations General Assembly had convened in New York. The U.N. had announced a plan for partition of Palestine with Jerusalem under U.N. trusteeship. The U.N. had also made a brave declaration of human rights and had adopted an indicting convention on poverty where it existed.

In Britain, Prince Charles had had his first birthday. George Orwell had written his prophetic *1984,* and Arthur Miller had produced his bitter and cryptic *Death of a Salesman.*

Few citizens of the region were inclined to spend their contemplative leisure reliving the last 130 years.

While Garrett set about organizing his resources, a representative of the Lewis Historical Publishing Company went about selling it. The history would be published in three volumes, with Garrett writing the first two books. The third book, which would use the flattering "mug" technique, would be made up of biographical sketches of leading men and women of the region. The price of the three-volume set would be $49.50. If the individuals who contracted for brief biographies wished to include a picture of themselves, the extra charge would be $200.

Garrett remembers that the Lewis representative in Atlanta was a crack salesman, past middle age, and an energetic worker.

In a few months fifteen hundred image-conscious Atlanta leaders had subscribed to the set. The third volume had already financed the entire undertaking. Garrett was encouraged by the report that Robert W. Woodruff, his boss at The Coca-Cola Company, had ordered twelve sets.

At that time Garrett was living in the Atlanta Historical Society's headquarters at Peachtree and Huntington Road. He had access to all the material the Society had amassed since its beginning in 1926. To that he would add the papers he had himself collected since his boyhood.

The earlier histories of Atlanta had been written chronologically up to a point, but then they veered off into chapters on special subjects—banking, churches, etc.—he had noticed.

"History evolves chronologically, of course. So I decided that I would write in that order. One can always go backward and forward. The first thing I did was to decide what pictures to use. . . . The Historical Society had a wealth of valuable pictures."

So to the amazement of his incredulous colleagues at Coca-Cola, Garrett proceeded to work his regular full-time hours, then rush back to the Historical Society to dig into Atlanta's roots. He worked every night, every weekend, every Sunday, pausing, he remembers now, only to dash out for a stimulating midnight cup of coffee at some nearby all-night rest stop.

Except among his friends, Garrett's project was not widely anticipated in Atlanta. "Nobody was holding his breath," was his laconic admission.

The first public acknowledgment of his undertaking apparently came on Thursday, November 22, 1951, when John Kiser began a feature article in the *Atlanta Constitution* with the statement that "Franklin Garrett, Atlanta businessman and historian, probably is about the only person who has read every newspaper in Atlanta since 1850."

Kiser first mentioned Garrett's necrology: "For more than twenty years he has been collecting facts about Atlanta's citizens in preparation of a gigantic list that will include every permanent white male resident of the area from 1820 to 1932.

"Ever since he wondered as a boy where the street he lived on began and where it ended, he has been a tireless historian. The next logical thing he was to find out was for whom the streets were named."

Kiser then mentioned the history on which Garrett had then been working for two years.

"But the history is a small task compared to compiling the list of Atlantans, a job which may take a lifetime. He is interested in where the city's people came from, what they accomplished here, and what became of them."

In that article the "tireless" Garrett was reported as bemoaning the fact that he could not get any court records before 1842 because that was the year the DeKalb County Courthouse burned to the ground. All the records were destroyed in the fire except the minute book of the Inferior Court, which later became the Court of Ordinary. The minute book was saved because the clerk of the court had taken it home to catch up on some work.

And on November 25, 1952, Garrett was married to Patricia Myhand Abbott of Birmingham, Alabama. Garrett was forty-six, his bride twenty-five. It was the first marriage for each.

Garrett moved his work from the bachelor quarters of the Historical Society to a new residential address at 3325 Paces Ferry Road, N.W.

There he continued his work, marshaling voluminous papers, printing the entire history in long hand. He had never learned to type, but he could print as fast as he could write. Lewis Historical Publishing Company agreed to settle for printing.

In early 1954, five years after he had begun his long chore, Garrett bundled up one hundred long yellow legal pads and sent them off to New York.

He had done what he had bargained to do. It was then in the publisher's hands.

In August 1954, as Atlanta was surging forward into its 120th year and was facing a volatile accommodation to desegregation under *Brown v. Board of Education*, fifteen hundred firmly packed boxes were delivered to the addresses of Atlanta's business, professional, and social leaders.

They contained two books, Volumes I and II, entitled *Atlanta and Environs—A Chronicle of Its People and Events* by Franklin M. Garrett, and a third volume, even more ponderous than the first two, entitled *Atlanta and Environs—A Chronicle of Its People and Events, Family and Personal History.* Altogether the books weighed more than ten pounds and consisted of something more than twenty-six hundred pages of copy, illustrative graphics, and indexes.

After a peremptory check to be sure their prepaid profiles had been reproduced, subscribers put the two weighty historical volumes aside for later perusal. There were important present matters to consider.

While Atlanta was wresting with the necessary accommodation to integration, Dr. Rufus Clement, the scholarly president of Atlanta University, decisively elected to the Board of Education of Atlanta, remarked: "It's a victory for the people. The white population is ready to work constructively with the Negro population."

A comprehensive new plan of improvement had just expanded the city's limits with vast opportunity for growth, and an alleged UFO had been glimpsed in a nearby town with space creatures emerging from a flying saucer. One of the creatures, allegedly captured, "looked like a hairless monkey," which, investigators admitted later, it turned out to be.

Atlanta and Environs was dedicated to the memory of Garrett's old friends and mentors, Walter McElreath, 1867-1951, and Beverly Means DuBose, Sr., 1886-1953, both of whom had led the young Garrett ever deeper into the thicket of regional Atlanta history. A grateful appreciation accompanied the dedication: "Without whose friendship, counsel and encouragement, the writing of this history of the community they loved so well, and to which they contributed so much, would not have been undertaken." It was signed with the initials F.M.G.

On the second page a preface acknowledged that "no historian, however diligent, can record the complete annals of even a single community. If he uses too small a brush, his picture is obscured by repetitious detail. If he undertakes to paint only in broad strokes, his pictures become a wide expanse, devoid of the interesting sidelights which bring the activities of human beings into focus. . . . I have made a consistent effort to achieve balance."

Continuing, Garrett especially thanked Miss Ruth Blair, then executive secretary of the Atlanta Historical Society, Wilbur G. Kurtz, Sr., for counsel and assistance in connection with the period of the War Between the States, Wilbur G. Kurtz, Jr., for his *Notes on the History of DeKalb County*, Allen P. Tankersley for the loan of useful materials, and Gordon F. Mitchell for his ever-ready willingness in furnishing information about early titles to Atlanta real estate.

Garrett also explained that both McElreath and DuBose, Sr., had read "most carefully" that part of the manuscript completed before their demise.

Further, a listing of twenty-seven persons, an advisory board, indicated that Garrett had not undertaken his assignment impetuously. They were: Beverly M. DuBose, Jr., Walter McElreath, Judge Stirling Price Gilbert, the Hon. William B. Hartsfield, Ivan Allen, Sr., James Walter Mason, John Ashley Jones, Miss Ruth Blair, Mrs. James E. Hays, Richard H. Rich, Stephens Mitchell, Frank Kells Boland, M.D., the Rev. Dr. Louie D. Newton, Charles A. Collier, the Hon. John M. Slaton, Ralph McGill, Wright Bryan, Henry A. Alexander, Charles P. King, Wilbur G. Kurtz, Sr., Mrs. Robert H. Jones, Jr., Gordon F. Mitchell, Hughes Spalding, Miss Ella May Thornton, Carl T. Hudgins, Mrs. Mark Temple, and Mrs. Ellis Arnall.

It was later remarked by an overawed observer, paraphrasing, "If these be for you, who can be against you?"

Garrett's references in *Atlanta and Environs* were overwhelming. All uses of material were footnoted at the end of each chapter and recapitulated in sources in a six-page bibliography.

The bibliography included 18 regional newspapers; 7 periodicals; 8 atlases, directories, and gazetteers; 26 pamphlets, booklets, and books; 24 legal and public documents and records; 158 general published sources; 5 manuscripts, including Garrett's own necrology collected over 25 previous years; and 9 unpublished manuscripts, including two doctoral dissertations in full binding.

The earliest newspapers were the *Milledgeville Southern Recorder,* 1825–1870; the *Columbus Times,* 1851; the *Columbus Southern Sentinel,* 1851–1852; and the Macon, Georgia, *Journal* and *Messenger,* 1853–1854. The only newspapers still in publication at that date (1954) (and presently are) were the *Atlanta Constitution* (1868) and the *Atlanta Journal* (1883).

The two volumes listed in its contents 136 illustrations and maps, including the Locomotive Florida arriving at Terminus in 1837. Terminus became Marthasville in 1843 and Atlanta in 1845.

The book, it turned out, did not open with drum rolls and flags waving. In a brief prelude to the "Coming of the White Men," Garrett acknowledged the explorer DeSoto, President James Monroe, and the Muscogee, Creek, and Cherokee Indians, who were to lose all their lands in this state in the conflict with the white men.

"It took one hundred and two years," Garrett recorded, "that is, from 1733 when the Creeks made a treaty at Savannah with Oglethorpe to 1835 when the Cherokees ceded the last of their territories in Northwest Georgia.

"The process took eighty-eight years until 1821 to reach the territory now occupied by Atlanta." (The controlling pressure: gold had been discovered in North Georgia, and the people of the state were pressing for speedy extinguishment of all remaining Indian titles.)

Garrett listed the sad, tolling Indian cessions of land, ever tightening and apparently inexorable: May 2, 1733, with General Oglethorpe; August 1, 1739, confirming the agreement of 1733; November 10, 1763, treaty negotiated at Augusta; June 1, 1773, another treaty at Augusta; August 7, 1790, a cession between Alexander McGillovray acting for the Creeks and Henry Knox, for the United States . . .

Continuing with the cessions from the Indians: June 1, 1802, all of nine present Georgia counties and five present towns; October 24, 1804, the "four-mile" purchase known as Wafford's entitlement; November 1805, land for Fort Hawkins, all of ten present counties and five present towns; August 9, 1814, the Creeks ceded the entire southwest portion of Georgia and much of lower Alabama to the redoubtable Gen. Andrew Jackson; July 8, 1817, the Cherokees ceded area around Wafford's settlement, comprising five counties and two towns; February 27, 1819, Cherokees ceded eight counties and two towns. (*Atlanta and Environs* was obviously not going to be a blithe book.)

Chapter 3 of the new history, dated 1825, included a heartbreaking letter from Jane Hawkins, daughter of William McIntosh, a man with both white and Indian parentage, great force of character, and noted chief of the Cowetas or Lower Creeks. He was also the first cousin to George M. Troup, governor of Georgia. McIntosh, under great duress, had signed a treaty at Indian Springs, Georgia, on behalf of the Creeks, which provided for the cession of all Creek territory in Georgia and Alabama in exchange for lands farther west.

The treaty served as McIntosh's death warrant. He was condemned to death, and the sentence was carried out on April 30, 1825, when a body of men went to his home, set fire to his house, riddled him with bullets, and suspended his scalp on a pile in a public square of Octuske, a Creek village.

Four days later, his daughter, Jane Hawkins, who was the widow of Col. Samuel Hawkins, wrote a pathetic letter to the U.S. Commissioners during the signing of the 1825 treaty. She wrote from Line Creek, Fayette County, May 3, 1825:

> If I had ten tongues I could not tell you all the truth. My father's house was surrounded by several hundred who murdered him, and took away the whole of father's money and property, leaving the family no clothes, not one rag, nor provision. . . . They were tying my husband with cords, to wait the arrival of the other execution which took place the same day and these barbarous men, not content with spilling the blood of both my husband and father to atone for their constant friendship to both your nation and our own, refused me the privilege of covering his body in the very ground which he had lately defended . . . drove me from my home, stript of all my property, my provision and my clothing with the painful reflection that the body of my poor murdered husband should remain unburied to be devoured by the birds and the beasts. . . . Was ever a poor woman worse off than I?"

Since presubscribed books are not available through ordinary book outlets and stores, and are not found for sale to the public, they are rarely reviewed by editors of book sections in periodicals.

Frank Daniel, Atlanta's foremost book reviewer of his time, however, recognized that this work merited attention.

Daniel wrote in the *Atlanta Journal:*

> These volumes should solve forever any question of "When did who do what?" in Atlanta from its beginnings to today, but it is highly improbable that this historian, at once exact and inexhaustible in tracking the wiliest fact to its lair, has overlooked a single detail. Franklin Garrett's timeless interest in the

background of his city has assembled a wealth of reliable information.

Mr. Garrett's history of *Atlanta and Environs* is presented in the first two of a three-volume set. Volume III, compiled by others, contains some 600 pages of biography and photographs of Atlantans, most of them contemporary and most of them well-to-do. This Volume III is entitled "Family and Personal History" and doubtless it had its special uses and special merits. But our review is concerned with the excellences of the two volumes, about 1,000 pages each, which Mr. Garrett has filled with the bold flow of Atlanta's history from the 1820s to the present. Here is at once a scholarly achievement and an invaluable contribution to the community. Under Mr. Garrett's astute and eagle-eyed investigation, surely no event and no incident of moment that ever happened in our environs has been allowed to get away.

Dr. Bell Wiley, professor of history at Emory University and author of *The Road to Appomattox* and other books on the Civil War, praised Garrett as "unsurpassed in his extensive knowledge of Atlanta's history."

And in their book *Georgiana,* a selection of a dozen collectible Georgia books, printed by Dan Abrams Co., Richard B. Harwell and Richard B. Willingham, Jr., included *Atlanta and Environs.* "This," they wrote, "is a local history, without equal, painstaking in detail, chronological in presentation, an incredible account of Atlanta's past. The third volume is subtitled 'Family and Personal History' and is a compilation of biographies of leading citizens."

Feature writers and columnists of the area seized upon the book and praised it in many accounts. They also discovered gems of humor, piquance, surprise, and horror they could purloin and expand for future essays. (This did not end in one year or several after publication.)

In one small clipping file in the Garrett collection, there are copies of columns by Ted Lippman in the *Constitution;* Yolande Gwin, several in the *Constitution;* John Kiser, *Atlanta Journal;* Edwin Holman, David Nordan, Dolores Irvin, Joe Cumming, Jr., Alan Patureau, Harold Martin, many over the years by Celestine Sibley, several by Norman Shavin, Midge Yearley, Bob Williman, and one or two by the writer of this book.

Every year since 1954 new talents on regional assignments have discovered Franklin Garrett anew, revealing once again his insights as if they had never been recognized before. He is gratified and amused by this attention. He finds their spin very refreshing.

It was many years before any hint of criticism of *Atlanta and Environs* began to be seen. The chief complaint was that it had no continuity, no sense of social development, and failed to look at things critically, to provide the sociology behind the chronology.

One writer said: "They say his history is inadequate and outmoded . . . the selection of a man who glories in the way things used to be for men like him and glosses over the way they were for others."

"Nonsense," observed his friend Virlyn B. Moore, Jr., who has been a history buff almost as long as Garrett. "He writes it as it is. He is not a revisionist. It is completely freed from a personal point of view. That's the way events were recorded."

Other supporters wrote indignant letters to the editor, and several wrote directly to Garrett. W. Elbridge Freeborn of Decatur wrote to the editor of the *Atlanta Weekly*, referring to an article published on Sunday, July 25, 1982: "I suspect that the authorities quoted might be professional historians, perhaps professional educators, but the suspicion lurks in my mind that Garrett's position, as Atlanta's most outstanding historian, galls them a bit.

"I think it is true that Garrett is not a professional historian by formal education, but he is a great historian of Atlanta by dint of his great interest and application."

Though Garrett is not prone to defend himself, he did react with annoyance "when those fellows want to express their ideas about sociology. That wasn't my point in writing a history of Atlanta. Contemporary accounts of events are reasonably accurate, because the reporters or observers are right on the ground at the time they are happening . . . so I put down the facts, as I could find them.

"And I have a line about *Atlanta and Environs* I have used many times. It is this: 'If it didn't happen, it is not in my books.'"

—— ∼ ——

DeKalb Notes

Garrett found the early personalities and domestic lives of DeKalb countians irresistible. Quoting from *Pioneers of DeKalb* by Albert Miles Hairston, published by the *DeKalb Standard* during the spring and summer of 1901, Garrett told of "'Merrell Collier who raised a nice family of children, all girls except one. His daughter, Charlotte, married the Hon. Eli J. Hulsey, who brought up a family of noble children. Col. T. J. Flake married their daughter, Laura. They too have brought up a family of bright, noble children. This makes three generations of Merrell Collier's descendants brought up on the old Collier Plantation.

"'Another old resident, Dr. Hayden Coe of Panole, married a second wife after his first wife died and left six or seven children. Two children blessed the second marriage. He had property, and when he was very old he divided it off to his first children what he intended them to have and kept back what he intended his wife and two other children to have. He then made a sale and sold off the surplus. . . .When they went to sell the horses, he had them brought up to the yard fence. They helped him out to the fence, and he cried like a child. It made him sad to part with his fine horses which he prized so highly. He knew he could not live a great while and seemed to want everything just to his notion while he lived. He was honest and upright in all his dealings. He was uneducated. He would not allow a man to impose on him. It is said that he never passed any words with a man, for it was a word and a blow, and the blow came first.'"

In discussing the origin of the name of Nancy Creek in Atlanta, Garrett found the following article from the *Atlanta Constitution* of Wednesday, January 31, 1883.

THE BIGGEST FAMILY

The widow of Mr. John L. Evins, late of this county, is living, stout and hearty. She is now 85 years old. She is the mother of 11 children, 57 grandchildren, and 93 great grandchildren. She settled with her husband on Nancy Creek in this county when the Indians were here. This creek is named for her. Mrs. Evins, the mother of J. C. Evins of this city, is still living at the old homestead settled 65 years ago. Who can beat that for an old inhabitant?

DeKalb County was "assented to" by Gov. John Clarke in another act on December 29, 1822, thus providing the machinery for organizing the county, wherein, slightly more than two decades later, the city of Atlanta was to rise and together with its suburbs spread itself over the land.

Garrett noted in passing: "Henry, Fayette and DeKalb Counties were all named for individuals prominent in the American Revolution. The first bears the name of Patrick Henry, Virginia orator and statesman, who accomplished so much in maintaining the morale of the colonists in their fight for independence; Fayette was named in honor of the Marquis de Lafayette, gallant French soldier, whose military aid to George Washington during the Revolution proved invaluable. The name of DeKalb County honors the memory of Baron Johann de Kalb, a native German, who made the supreme sacrifice upon behalf of American freedom at the battle of Camden, S.C., August 9, 1780."

DeKalb, at that time, claimed approximately twenty-five hundred persons. These original settlers were plain people, primarily of English, Scotch, and Irish descent. They came mostly from Virginia, North Carolina, and South Carolina. For the most part the pioneers were poor and meagerly educated, but they were generally industrious and temperate, qualities needed in the wilderness they sought to conquer. Their original homes were usually log cabins, owner-built and occupied. The unit of land ownership was primarily one land lot of 202 acres. The individual ownership of slaves was small. Possession of a dozen or more was the exception rather than the rule, and the majority of the early citizens, down to the time of the Emancipation Proclamation, owned none or, at the most, one or two house servants. Large plantations, such as were known in the older East and Middle Georgia counties, did not exist in early DeKalb.

——— — ———

Mulligan Ball

Garrett could not resist recording an interview that appeared in the *Atlanta Constitution* with John J. Thrasher in 1897 relative to Thrasher's early experiences at Terminus, the tentative designation for Atlanta.

Thrasher's account of the first social function (and the first labor trouble) in the community has become one of the favorite anecdotes of the million words of *Atlanta and Environs*:

"I was building the Monroe Embankment for the W&A mainline in 1839. My foreman was a man named Mulligan. He was a good workman. Mulligan was Irish, a married man, and so were others of my laborers, most of whom lived in the neighborhood of the present Presbyterian Church. These shacks were rude cabins made from roughly sawed timber. All of them had dirt floors. There was not a plank floor among them all.

"Mrs. Mulligan heard that the shacks were not floored with boards, and she refused to move down here with her husband unless her cabin was floored with planks. She was the foreman's wife, and she felt that she was entitled to something better than a dirt floor. There was nothing for me to do but to buy the lumber and put a wooden floor in the Mulligan shack, and I had to go out to Collier's mill for the material. Well, I bought a load or two of puncheon and laid the best floor I could for Mrs. Mulligan.

"No sooner was she installed in her new home than she announced she would give a ball. The wives of all the other men working on the railroad were invited, and they all came.

"The first society of Atlanta was there, and it was a swell affair. Mrs. Mulligan was mistress of ceremonies, and she said that I would have to dance the first set with her. I had on a pair of rough high-topped boots, but that gave Mrs. Mulligan no concern. She said it didn't matter at all. We circled around a few times, and the heel of one of my boots got caught in the floor and the heel came off. I finished the dance in a hippity-hop sort of fashion, but, as they say nowadays, everything went then. It was a crème de la crème affair, and the function established Mrs. Mulligan as the leader of the four hundred. She was a fine looking woman of strong physique, and if anybody had questioned her leadership she could have established her claim to the championship as well as to the leadership.

"But you know how women are about things. If one has something her neighbor wants it too. Well, sir, the day after the ball a delegation of the men came to me and announced that their wives wanted plank floors in their shacks, and that if I didn't put them in the houses every blessed man of them would quit work.

"I had to send out to Collier's mill and get a good many loads of puncheons to floor the other shacks. That is the history of the first social function that ever occurred in Atlanta (then Terminus) after the Indians left this county.

"The smart set has changed a good deal in the years which have elapsed since Mrs. Mulligan's ball, but I bet they never enjoyed a dance more than that first one was enjoyed."

CHAPTER 12

The Civil War, from Atlanta and Environs, with Garrett's Later Account of Atlanta's Surrender and Rebirth

Garrett devoted 192 pages to the Civil War—100,000 words, the length of an ordinary book—in four chapters. He used 525 footnotes.

Chapter 39, dated 1861, began:

> Atlanta, as has been seen, experienced a remarkable career of growth and business prosperity thus far in its history. But when the first sounds of war's alarms were heard throughout the land, the march of uninterrupted progress diverged from its accustomed course and sought new and hitherto untried channels. Normal building operations were . . . discontinued. Population, however, steadily increased and business, in unaccustomed channels, acquired an astonishing vigor and grew to immense proportions.
>
> Atlanta was soon to become one of the chief military centers and supply depots of the Confederacy, and ere long a major objective of Federal armies.

The details from many sources of the "dreadful" war followed: letters, votes for and against secession, grand jury presentments, officers and noncoms of all fighting companies in Fulton County, Atlanta city minutes, ordinances, deaths in battle, punishments (hangings), county officers, city council meetings, military notes and orders, advertisements, diaries, plagues, wounded soldiers, exhibitions, wartime prices, warnings, presidential visit, maps, court minutes, opposing Federal forces, militia notices, new churches, military directory, exchanges of generals' messages, movement of troops, special field orders from both sides, strategies, weather, casualties of the Battle of Atlanta, Lorena's "Song of Defeat," destruction ("the earth trembled)," refugees ("What will become of us, God only knows)," losses in Atlanta campaign: Union, 31,687; Confederate 34,979; a list of street and house destruction, return of citizens from exile, and the concluding paragraphs:

> These and other returning citizens found their beloved city a picture of abject desolation. . . . They gazed upon tumble-down walls enclosing masses of loose brick, fragments of tin roofing blocked the streets and became entangled in the wheels of vehicles. Blackened chimneys rose starkly, the red clay fortifications stood out in bold relief. Here and there, emerging from a corner of some ruined building where a mass of tin roofing had been placed to afford a wretched abode were seen Negro children clad only in tow sacks with openings at the corners for armholes. And everywhere were lean and hungry dogs and cats, searching and fighting over stray scraps of food.
>
> It was a prospect to discourage all but the most determined. Yet hope springs eternal and with a total of $1.64 in the city treasury (according to the report of J. H. Mecaslin, late City Treasurer, to the Mayor and City Council of Atlanta), and visions of a greater city, coupled with the immediate necessity of earning a living, the returning citizens doffed their coats, rolled up their sleeves and went to work.

By Christmas day, at least one of the amenities was enjoyed, when Dr. Henry C. Hornady preached the first post-war sermon at the First Baptist Church. It was a message of hope and prophecy.

And so we find Atlanta, at the end of its year of greatest travail, not happy, not prosperous and by no means intact, but at least alive and with hope for a better future.

Garrett mused about the city of Atlanta at the time of its surrender and burning.

"Atlanta has always had drama, no doubt about that. How many cities have undergone three major battles within the city limits, and then surrender to an invading army, plus the burning, or dynamiting, of practically all of its infrastructure?

"Now, you will hear people say that Atlanta was completely burned out, that there wasn't anything left. That's erroneous. Mainly the residences were spared. The object of the Union Army was to destroy the industry, which helped keep the Confederacy going. That was their object, to destroy the industry and force it to surrender, which it did a little later.

"The history of Atlanta from 1837 until its surrender during the Civil War was one of progress, all the way. In 1850, for instance, the population of Atlanta (which was still in DeKalb County) was approximately twenty-five hundred. Then you moved up to the next census year, 1860, and it had increased to about eight thousand and was no longer in DeKalb County. One of the great steps forward, as far as Atlanta was concerned, was to become a county in its own name. That occurred in December 1853, when Fulton County was created, practically all out of DeKalb County, and that necessitated a courthouse and more public officials, etc.

"The city continued to grow in the 1850s very fast, as indicated by the difference in population. The war years, of course, were pretty rugged, and in 1864 the population of Atlanta was around fifteen thousand with many transients coming and going. Two or three newspapers moved here from Tennessee, where they couldn't publish. They came here and published for a time.

"Then, of course, the city finally surrendered to the Union Army. That took place on September 2, 1864. During August of 1864, Sherman was getting very impatient about capturing Atlanta. He had already fought three battles and was still not in Atlanta.

"Sherman's strategy as he came south was not to attack the very strong fortification of Atlanta by sending waves of men against them to be shot down. His strategy was to capture and put out of commission the four railroads serving Atlanta. That meant tearing up enough tracks so they couldn't operate. So that became his principal objective, and he came down the Western and Atlantic . . . the one that was here in the first place. Now it is known as the CSX transportation company main line from here to Chattanooga. It was the southern supply line south and Sherman's supply line north. So he decided to cut out the railroad.

"The eyes and ears of the army in those days was the cavalry. They didn't have airplanes then, and the use of balloons was very limited and not very successful. The cavalry would reconnoiter and then report back to the head man. Sherman wanted to get around to the east of Atlanta, because if Lee could have provided any reinforcements from the Army of Virginia (which he couldn't do, but Sherman didn't know that), they would have to come in on the Georgia Railroad from Augusta. So Sherman was trying to get around to the north side of Atlanta. His army crossed the Chattahoochee River, on all of the ferries upriver from Bolton, where the Water Works are now located. He decided on that so he could maneuver around the east side of Atlanta and cut the Georgia railroad somewhere.

"He had already taken over the W&A as he came down. . . . That was in the bag, as he advanced. The Battle of Peachtree Creek occurred on July 20. It was fought way outside of town. That battle was indecisive. Meanwhile, the Confederate command had changed. General Johnston had been relieved of the command of the Southern Army by Jefferson Davis (the two men didn't like each other much anyway), and General Hood, a much younger man, was put in command.

"Hood took his command as an order to get out and fight. Johnston didn't have much fight because his army was outnumbered, about half the size of Sherman's, and could easily be outflanked. Anyhow, the Battle of

Atlanta was fought on July 22, two days after the Battle of Peachtree Creek.

"Meanwhile, Union cavalry had managed to get around to the east of Atlanta, and cut the tracks of the Georgia Railroad, tear up enough of it so it couldn't operate. If Lee could have spared any reinforcements to Johnston and Hood, they would have come in that way.

"The Battle of Atlanta was the largest of the three fought in the city limits. It resulted in many casualties, but it didn't open the gates for Sherman to get in quite yet.

"Meanwhile, there were still two railroads that were operating: the Atlanta and West Point, and the Central of Georgia. They came in over a joint right-of-way from East Point. Sherman felt that if he could get to Atlanta, he would have it in the bag. That didn't work out. He fought the Battle of Ezra Church, in the present Westview Cemetery area.

"It was definitely a Union victory, but it still didn't get him into Atlanta. Meanwhile, his cavalry had succeeded in getting to the Atlanta and West Point Railroad at Red Oak. They tore up enough tracks to put it out of business for a while. The Macon and Western, which later became the Central of Georgia down to Macon and Savannah, was still running, and as long as it was, Atlanta could be supplied. So in desperation Sherman subjected Atlanta to an artillery bombardment all during August 1864. He planted big guns at high points around Atlanta and lobbed artillery shells, and nobody knew where they were going to fall or when. It must have been a frightening place to live at that time. The bombardment caused many casualties and much property damage.

"At the end of August, Sherman withdrew from Atlanta. He still didn't know where he was going. He retreated to the south, down to Clayton County. His destiny was Jonesboro. He got opposite Fairburn and moved across Clayton County where the airport is now and showed up at Jonesboro, where the Battle of Jonesboro was fought.

"That was a Federal victory without any question. It resulted in Sherman's controlling all four railroads, so General Hood saw the jig was up. He didn't bother to surrender the city to anybody. To use a modern term, he just scratched off. His army went down to about Lovejoy.

"Meanwhile, Mayor James M. Calhoun, a lawyer in Atlanta who had been practicing since 1850 or thereabouts, was ready to surrender the city, but there wasn't anybody to surrender it to. So he assembled some of the leading citizens, plus councilmen, and they all met at Five Points and decided to ride out Marietta Street showing a flag of truce, in order to find some responsible Federal units to whom to surrender Atlanta. They were unarmed. They finally surrendered Atlanta where Northside Drive crosses Marietta Street.

"Mayor Calhoun was one of the forty-seven men who have served as mayor of Atlanta, and the only one . . . hopefully will remain so . . . to have surrendered Atlanta to an invading army.

"Sherman decided to give his army a rest. They'd had a tough campaign, so they settled in for two and a half months. And, of course, human nature always comes to the fore, so the highest officers in the Union Army occupied the best houses in Atlanta during the time they were here. It is worthy of note that none of those houses were destroyed.

"As I've said here before, anybody that says Atlanta was completely destroyed . . . wiped off the map . . . they're all wet.

"The industries were destroyed, very much so. The Union Army occupied Atlanta until mid-November, when they departed to the sea—their March to the Sea. The citizens who had been expelled from the city began to come back and rebuild.

"Meanwhile, Sherman got to Savannah about Christmas. They didn't offer any resistance. It would have been futile to do so. And that sewed up Lincoln's run for the presidency. He needed a definitive victory. So Atlanta suffered more damage than any other city in the Civil War except Richmond, Virginia, and Columbia, S.C. Of course, war is wholesale vandalism anyway.

"The citizens of Atlanta didn't stand on ceremony. They began to come back as well as they could. The city was no longer occupied by Federal troops. The gates were wide open. They began to rebuild. . . . Atlanta, Richmond, and Columbia were unique in having to rebuild . . . and I think it shows the fiber of their people. They didn't just give up and mope around. They exhibited more of a Rhett Butler attitude than an Ashley Wilkes attitude. So we've got to rebuild. Of course we couldn't do it overnight . . . material was short. But it was accomplished, and by 1870, only six years after the war ended, the census showed that Atlanta had leaped up to twenty-two thousand residents.

"Of course it involved black people. They were now free and weren't tied down to cotton plantations or other agricultural duties, and freedom meant a change of scenery.

"A great many black people began to settle in certain neighborhoods. . . . Most of those were not on high ground. . . . A good many of the early black settlements were in the valleys. . . . Atlanta is kind of a series of valleys and hills anyway. Many black people had learned trades, blacksmithing, plastering, carpentry, and that stood everyone in good stead."

——— — ———

The Civil War Round Table

Many of the notes used in the writing of the Civil War account in *Atlanta and Environs* had been gleaned by Garrett himself, who with Beverly DuBose, Sr., and Jr., and others had spent years of weekends and Sundays searching through country courthouse records, old cemeteries, and mainly old battlefields for memorabilia and artifacts of all sorts.

When the writing was finished on the *Atlanta and Environs* manuscript and it had been sent off to the publisher the four men decided that the Civil War required continued scrutiny. Richard Harwell, Beverly DuBose, Jr., Wilbur Kurtz, Jr., and Garrett organized the Atlanta chapter of the Civil War Round Table. The Round Table was founded for the purpose of holding monthly meetings from September until hot weather in the summer, just to talk about the Civil War. Garrett is the only member of the original quartet still living.

The organization has grown to more than one hundred members in 1996. They once met at restaurants, but they now meet at the Ansley Golf Club, with a set program and a featured speaker. "We are not just interested in the Atlanta campaign, but the whole war. So that gives our meetings more scope," Garrett explained.

Garrett was president of the Civil War Round Table in 1962 and 1963, and over the years he has made talks on such subjects as "The Battle of Ezra Church," "Life inside Wartime Atlanta," "The Part Played by the Railroads in the Civil War," "The Atlanta Campaign" (with Col. Ned Julian), "Atlanta in 1866," "Atlanta, 1865," "Atlanta in 1861." He was the host for a tour of the new Historical Society archives by the Round Table group on June 10, 1975. He was also featured on Franklin Garrett night on February 14, 1989, as the honorary member of the Atlanta Civil War Round Table.

——— — ———

Turning Points

Garrett wanted to talk about other events that changed the course of history in Atlanta—"turning points," he said, that set a new direction.

"The public schools were organized and formally opened in 1872. The first public school was the Ivy School. It was on the east side of Ivy between Cain and Harris, where the Ivan Allen Company headquarters are now located. I remember the old Ivy Street school. It was a frame building well back from the street. The area between the school building and the street was just a playground.

"Several other schools opened about the same time . . . Crew Street and Walker Street and a Boys High and a Girls High. They were set up right downtown in buildings that were already there. They were later moved into larger buildings, but the point I am making is that we got our school system going in 1872, and it has continued to grow ever since that.

"Schools were segregated by race and at the high school level by sex. That continued for many years. I myself went to old Tech High. The main building is still standing on Luckie Street. It was a run-down campus, to say the least. We had buildings on Luckie Street, Marietta Street, Simpson Street, and Latimer Street. The old run-down buildings on Latimer Street were called by the boys 'The Million Dollar Building' and 'The Billion Dollar Annex Building.' They were not in very good repair.

"Schools were separate for black children. We didn't get a black high school until 1925, with the founding of the Booker T. Washington High School on Ashby Street. It was a fine building.

"Tech High was in a neighborhood you couldn't call a society neighborhood at all. It was in an industrial area, and west of the high school was Marietta Street, then the railroad tracks, factories on the other side of the tracks, and on the east side was a fairly modest neighborhood, a blue-collar street along Simpson and Venable and Fowler . . . all those streets.

"We got boys from all over Atlanta, from the tough spots like Bellwood, etc., to the more genteel ones like Ansley Park. I don't remember a single instance of any student coming to school with a pistol or a knife large enough to do any damage to anyone. It wasn't done.

"Boys High, for many years, was at Courtland and Gilmer Streets. It had more of a classical curriculum. Tech High had shop courses, but it also had English, spelling, history, geography, etc., where the boys learned a trade. I think I got a pretty good education there. Of course, the reason I chose Tech High is that the boys I ran around with decided to go there. That's about as deep as your investigation goes when you are that age.

"In 1875 we finally got running water. Prior to that time Atlanta had been an outdoor-plumbing town; only two or three or maybe four of the private dwellings had running water inside. It was supplied by cisterns in the back yard or the water was pumped up through the house.

"Running water was a great asset to the volunteer fire department. Prior to that time Atlanta firemen had to work from cisterns. There would be a fire call. They would go to the nearest cistern, hoping it wasn't too far away from the fire, and pump water onto the fire. I might point out that the Atlanta Fire Department was volunteer until 1882, when Atlanta became just too large for a volunteer fire department.

"Water was a great boon to the city. The first works were not where they are now. When the system was first established, the city bought up the Terry Mill property, which is where Lakewood is now. It was a nice acreage, and there was water of good quality available there . . . but after they got it built, they found there just wasn't enough of it. The city was growing very fast. So they labored with that for several years and then in the middle 1880s decided to augment the supply by drilling an artesian well at Five Points. That was drilled. I think they went down to about three thousand feet. . . . They must have thought they were going to China before they struck enough water for it to amount to anything. When they did get water, the quality was not very good. It was a help. But after they got under way with this, the Health Department decided the water was not fit for human consumption. They wanted to use it, so they piped it around to downtown business water troughs because all transportation in those days was by animal power . . . mules and horses which got thirsty.

"Finally, in 1893, the Water Works were moved to where they are now . . . to Hemphill Avenue and Fourteenth Street, where they had a big pumping system . . . station . . . with the settling tanks along Howell Mill Road. The main water plant was out where Peachtree Creek flows into the Chattahoochee River, where it still is. So we moved out there in 1893, and it was adequate. It was good water, plenty of it, and particularly with the building of the Buford Dam as the years went on. So we had running water and were more of a city than a country town.

"The next amenity was the telephone. Alexander Graham Bell invented that in 1876, and it was a great boon, though at first people didn't know how to handle it. The first telephone conversation in Atlanta was between the ticket office of the W&A Railroad and the Union Station, a distance of two or three blocks. They could have hollered out a window, I guess.

"The earliest telephone directory is a one-page publication. I believe it was 1881, and most of the subscribers were business firms. It didn't appeal to too many homes at first, but a little later, just about everybody joined in.

"Now, if one were to pick up all the telephone directories at once, one would be straining a back.

"The city was first lighted with gas in 1855, when the company was organized to furnish gas to the city. The city bought ornamental lamp posts, fifty of them, and installed them around the business section. The purpose of the gas then was strictly for illumination. Not for cooking or anything else . . . and the posts provided a convenient place for a fellow who was a little bit drunk on the way home to lean on.

"The Atlanta Gas Light Company was incorporated in 1856 and is our oldest corporation, with the exception of one or two of the railroads which antedated everything else. So now we had gas.

"Electricity was tried on a tentative basis around about 1886. George Hillyer was mayor of Atlanta in 1884 and 1885, and they tried lighting the streets with electricity. The cost for the whole year was about $3,500, which Mr. Hillyer considered too high. He announced that if the owners did not see fit to lower the rates, we might decide just to go with gas. Anyway, electricity began its long career in Atlanta both with streetcars and electric lights.

"The Georgia Railway and Power Company was organized in 1902. It supplied electric lights and transportation to the city. The Georgia Power Company was called the Georgia Railway and Power Company until they sold the transportation part of the company in 1950. . . . Then they ceased to furnish transportation.

"The two principal founders were Harry M. Atkinson and Preston S. Arkwright. Mr. Atkinson started off as chairman of the board. He held that office until he died in 1939. Mr. Arkwright served as president from 1902 until his retirement, I believe, in 1945.

"So our public utilities were getting under way . . . utilities that any major city had to have if it was going to be of any importance.

"The first serious race riot we had here in Atlanta was on September 22 and 23, 1906. At that time we had a newspaper published here by W. R. Hearst. It was called the *Atlanta Georgian*—started in 1906. It was

Harry M. Atkinson (1862-1939) with Enrico Caruso (r), ca. 1910. Photo courtesy of the Atlanta History Center

inclined to be somewhat sensational. It reported several attacks, whether they were carried out, I don't know . . . black men on white women on the outskirts of the city. That, of course, inflamed the kind of people who would start a riot, and we had one that was very serious . . . which was started by a young white man.

"In town the rowdies would assault black people. . . . One man, a barber, was killed in his shop, and a couple of the waiters at the Union Station got away the best they could. They (the rioters) even got into the Pullman car and pulled the porters out. I think the total casualties were about twelve, mostly black people, but also included two or three policemen. That was the worst one we have ever had, and it caused the city fathers to pause and think about matters.

"Blacks then got the right to vote, and in the 1950s, the racial legislation was passed . . . giving them the right to do the things they couldn't do heretofore. They could sit down on a streetcar whenever they wanted to and not just at the back of it. They no longer had 'Black' and 'White' water fountains, and they could also eat in public restaurants.

"Prior to the Civil War, it had been against the law to teach black people to read and write . . . and what they needed more than anything else was some education. That led to the founding of the black colleges here . . . namely Atlanta University. It was founded by the Freedman's Aid Society for the purpose of giving the freedmen education. Of course it wasn't Atlanta University at college level when it started off . . . but Atlanta University was the first of its kind. There were a number of black colleges founded in Atlanta down to the turn of the century.

"Atlanta University was followed in the next ten or twelve years by Spelman, Morehouse, Gammon Theological, Morris Brown, Clark University, and the others. They weren't all on the west side at that time. That is a very interesting section of Atlanta. Gammon and Clark were on the south side. Morris Brown was on the east side, over on Boulevard and Houston. They all finally got together on the west side.

"Atlanta's greatest travail, of course, was the destruction in the Civil War. As I have said before, many of the leaders of the city were northern men, who were inclined to be more energetic than any of the southern gentlemen, who moved around somewhat more slowly.

"The South was really agricultural, but beginning after the war, it gradually became more industrial and had to go on developing more than just agriculture.

"So we went through that. It was pretty tough. I have often thought if I could be carried back to Atlanta in that time . . . with the knowledge I have now . . . how interesting that would be . . . the contrast between the construction—the reconstruction really, following the war, and the present-day progress.

"In the five-year period between 1865 and 1870, the state capital was moved to Atlanta. The state had adopted a new constitution in 1868, and one of the provisions was that the state capitol would be moved from Milledgeville to Atlanta. It had been at Milledgeville since 1807. Milledgeville was right in the middle of Georgia—and it was felt that was where the capitol should be. (There was much more population to the east than there was to the north.) So the capital was moved here. Milledgeville didn't like it much. The reason was there was more going on here. Milledgeville was not on a main line railroad and didn't have good passenger service, or freight service either, even though it was in the middle of the state.

"There were several other abortive efforts to move the capital to Macon, which was bigger than Milledgeville. Macon is also very near the middle of the state, but that didn't get to first base.

"In addition to getting the capitol moved here in that five-year period . . . the Constitution of 1868 enabled women to control their own property. Prior to that time a woman could marry some bum, and he could sell off her property and drink it all up and gamble it away, and she had no recourse, but after 1868 she could control her own property. That was a great step forward.

"The *Atlanta Constitution* newspaper was born in 1868. The first edition appeared on June 16 of that year. Up to that time Atlanta had been sort of a burying ground for unsuccessful newspapers and that continued up through the 1880s, more or less. I think that men who want to edit a newspaper are better at that than they are at financing it. Most of them went broke. The *Constitution* survived and is still going strong.

"In the way of retail shopping, a young man named Morris Rich, a young fellow from Hungary, came to Atlanta in 1867 and founded a little department store on Whitehall Street in a wooden building. It all grew up to be a giant in size, known far and wide as Rich's.

"So you see we didn't just lie down and cry . . . we rebuilt the city. By 1870, many of the scars of the war still existed around the city and the country, but those were gradually eliminated.

"The city of Atlanta, during the 1870s, acquired more of the amenities than it had heretofore enjoyed. Incidentally, the railroads were all back in order and running by 1865. They didn't lose any time. Transportation has always been Atlanta's lifeblood . . . roads, railroads, air transportation, and water.

"The Chattahoochee River, which is the source of our water supply, has never been navigable from here to Columbus. . . . It is from Columbus on down, but not by big ships.

"But by 1871 Atlanta got public transportation in the form of horse-car lines, provided to the city by Richard Peters and George W. Adair. Adair had already founded the real estate business . . . Adair Realty Company. Richard Peters was one of Atlanta's pioneer citizens, who had come here from Philadelphia. He bought up land, became one of our largest land owners, and was altogether a very valuable citizen.

"He and his wife in 1881 built a large home on Peachtree on land he had bought in 1849 . . . and lived there the last eight years of his life until he died in 1889. That house was on the site of the First Baptist Church. His widow continued to live in the house until her death in 1911.

"Peters and Adair were two very active businessmen. Peters was a little more adept at handling his money than Adair, but anyway they established the streetcar system, which was on iron rails.

"Atlanta was difficult to walk around in . . . in wet weather or dry weather . . . either seas of mud or clouds of dust. So that was a big help to the growth of the city. . . . It could go out a little further. Again, human nature comes to the fore.

"The first streetcar line the city got running was the West End. That ran right by the Peters home, which at that time was at the intersection of the street which bears his name and Forsyth Street. Then it continued out Peters to West End to where Mr. Adair lived, so the first line served their house.

"And another line ran out from Decatur to Oakland Cemetery, and another ran out McDonough Avenue, now Capitol Avenue, which was a very up-and-coming residential section. Another ran out Peachtree Street to North Avenue. The first electric streetcars did not come into being in Atlanta until Joel Hurt's time in the late 1880s, when he was developing Inman Park.

"However, Atlanta was served by a number of other streetcar companies, in addition to the original ones. They had lines more or less all over town, going out to Grant Park and other localities. The first line ran from Inman Park to what is now Five Points, but the other lines remained horse cars until 1894. By that time the horse cars, or hayburners, as they were called, had ceased to exist.

"One of the last horse cars sat in the yard of the Healey family home on the northeast corner of Auburn Avenue and Ivy Street, where the telephone company building now is. The Healey family had been founded here by Thomas G. Healey, who was the grandfather of the two brothers, William and Oliver, who were both very valuable citizens of Atlanta."

CHAPTER 13

Who Can Stump Franklin?

For fifty-six years, one of the rites of spring in Atlanta has been a light-hearted little civic revel called "Stumping Franklin Garrett."

Such a stumping was announced again in March 1996, with the expected results. As Paula Crouch of the *Atlanta Journal* wrote in 1983, "History buffs turned out in droves, packing the parking lot and spilling out onto Andrews Drive with their cars, filling nearly every seat in McElreath Hall." Dozens of other writers and commentators have described the ritual event in their own ways in the intervening years.

The first "Stumping Garrett," on June 9, 1940, was a feature in the *Atlanta Constitution Sunday Magazine*. It was published under the headline "Do You Know Atlanta? Another Quiz on Facts about the City's Growth."

The article announced the guest conductor as an "Atlanta Advertising Executive considered one of the city's foremost historical experts . . . widely known for his genealogical work, author of several historical articles and historical compilations in the *Atlanta Historical Bulletin*, the Atlanta Society's quarterly, and to the Atlanta newspapers."

This rave introduction was published when Garrett was thirty-four and vice president of the Atlanta Historical Society, long before he had emerged as the author of his magnum opus *Atlanta and Environs*, which cinched his title in several historical directories.

Franklin M. Garrett with publications of the Atlanta Historical Society, 1986. William F. Hull, photographer. Photo courtesy of the Atlanta History Center

The first published interrogation included twenty-five questions, with answers in a subsequent section. It was illustrated with a serious-faced Garrett, looking more professorial than his years. He had just begun his work with The Coca-Cola Company.

The printed questions were flattering to Atlanta's past: "Where was the residence of Woodrow Wilson during the time he practiced law in Atlanta in 1882 and 1883? . . . What Atlantan served as Secretary of the Interior? . . . Who was the first President of the United States to visit Atlanta? . . . What was John S. Pemberton's chief claim to distinction?"

Through the following years, the patterns of stumping have changed somewhat. So has the crowd of attendants. The friends of Garrett who come now may be the grandchildren of his original audiences. They have inherited this handsome icon from their ancestors.

Nowadays two lecterns are set, one at each end of the speaker's platform. On the left side an assistant stands in place. For a long time James Landon, trustee of the Atlanta History Center and a younger attorney friend of the Garretts, has been in the "Mr. Interlocutor" role. The afternoon is free, of course.

The ticket for admission is one question for Garrett. These slips of paper are collected and taken to James Landon. Landon reads them, smiles knowingly, tauntingly, then hands one of them to the suave gentleman standing comfortably at his right for his answer.

Garrett is as easy at the lectern as he is in his own home. He looks at the paper and thinks.

"This question," he reads, his powerful baritone voice sounding a little raveled at the edges, "asks if I know the name of the doorman at Davison's department store. Well, of course that store has been Macy's for a long time, you know. So I must ask the writer . . . which door of Macy's are you interested in?"

Another question. "This is digging back into the 1930s, but do you know the name of Bobby Jones's famous putter?"

Answer: "Mmmmmm. . . . Well, I'm not much of a golfer, never have been, but I think his putter's name was Calamity Jane. Don't know how he won with that name."

Question: "Mr. Garrett, what is the age of Stone Mountain (Atlanta's great granite landmark)?"

Pause. Garrett has become slightly hard of hearing, and he appears to ponder for a moment. "Well, now, Stone Mountain is very old. Very old, indeed. And it is about the only landmark that hasn't been moved anywhere else in our city."

The audience leans on each question and answer as if they were lines from Shakespeare. Little gasps of amusement, of loving wonder. Whispers and nudgings from one seat to the next.

Over the years, Garrett has answered thousands of questions, not all of them trivial by any means.

Then the lights come back on. Depending on the cleverness and interest of the questions, it has been a fascinating hour or so. Applause . . . applause. Everyone stands, as they had when Garrett made his entrance.

He walks out briskly, sturdy, confident, polite, nodding in acknowledgment and pleasure. He knows the game. So do they. It is an exchange of friendship. Many of them speak to him as he passes their aisles. "He was a friend of my grandfather," whispers one man to his neighbor. "They were in school together."

It is quite a reunion. Really an homage, as everybody knows.

CHAPTER 14

Since 1902, the Atlanta Symposium

Since 1942, Franklin Garrett has been a member of a venerable old organization called Symposium, the Symposium, Atlanta Symposium, and the Atlanta Symposium, which began back in 1902.

A chit from the Piedmont Driving Club dated March 17, 1942, probably marked an awakening of Garrett's interest. It read:

10 dinners at $1.50 . . . . $15.00

3 cigars . . . . $ .38

The early records show that the Symposium, whatever its agreed-upon name, was composed of a group of men "who see each other in two of the great activities of life, eating and thinking. Let me see a man eat and let me know how and what he is thinking and I will tell you what he is."

At the organization of the club and for a short time thereafter, when the refreshments were limited to a plate of crackers and a bottle of wine, the motto was "Plain Living and High Thinking."

But soon the volume of the refreshments was increased, and by tacit consent the motto was changed to "High Living and Any Old Kind of Thinking." The existing notes continued

The club members shall assemble promptly at 6:30 P.M. At that hour the front door shall be locked and barred and all members not present shall forfeit all their interest in the grub of the evening.

If a late member tries to storm the door or break in a window, he shall be arrested for burglary.

The eats shall be on the table at 6:30. If they are not, it shall not be considered breach of etiquette for the guests to mob the cook and help themselves.

One and one-half hours shall be allowed for eating and thirty minutes for the essay. When the essay begins, the secretary shall move his chair to the essayist's side. The secretary shall be armed with a stopwatch in one hand and a rolling pin in the other. At the exact second the thirty minutes expire, he shall cave in the essayist with the pin and roll him under the table. This procedure is established for the double purpose of stopping the essayist on time, and keeping him from butting in while the general discussion is going on.

To these noble by-laws some of Atlanta's finest scholars subscribed with membership to the Symposium. The lists, going back to charter members, include judges, doctors, lawyers, merchants, professors, editors, ministers, philanthropists, artists, university presidents, senators, legislators, military officers, psychiatrists, international business moguls, librarians, writers, architects, and assorted intellectuals.

Eighteen stellar citizens comprised the charter members: Judge Joseph Lumpkin, Dr. David Marx, Dr. C. B. Wilmer, Dr. A. W. Stirling, Samuel D. Jones, Walter G. Cooper, Dr. J. C. Olmsted, Joseph C. Logan, Linton C. Hopkins, Rev. M. L. Troutman, H. A. Arbuckle, George Muse, Henry C. Peeples, the Rev. C. A. Langston, Judge Alex C. King, A. V. Gude, Dr. Stiles Bradley, a Dr. Sanborn, and Judge Joseph Lamar.

In 1906, six men had discoursed on the following erudite subjects: "The Miracle of Growth," L. C. Hopkins; "The Monroe Doctrine," Judge Joseph Lumpkin; "The Bible and Modern Thought," Dr. David Marx; "Naturalism and Supernaturalism," George Muse; "Brain and Personality," Dr. D. C. Olmsted; and "Parasites and Cranks," Dr. C. B. Wilmer.

In Garrett's early time, 1942 and onward, the subjects were far from frivolous: "The Vanishing Trail of the Cherokee," Dr. Edward G. Mackay; "South America," Albert Staton; "Pleasantries of the Younger Pliny," William Cole Jones; "The Great Cosmic Urge," Linton Hopkins; "The Devil," Dr. Harvey W. Cox; "The Doctor of 1850," Dr. Dan Elkin; "Grandpa's Book," Wright Bryan; "An Hour with Walt Whitman," Linton Hopkins; "A Sophist," Philip Weltner; "William Byrd of Westover and Wife," The Rev. Edward G. Mackay; "Between the Testaments," Dean Raimundo de Ovies; "Kings and Queens of Waverly," William Cole Jones; "Poets," Thomas Hopkins English.

The Symposium still meets regularly. Meetings are held in members' homes or at their clubs, whichever is their preference. The present members are: Bond Almand, Jr., James G. Bogle, Dr. Robert L. Brown, Tom Watson Brown, Colin Campbell, Franklin Garrett, Pegram Harrison, Henry Howell, Wilbur Kurtz, Jr., James A. Mackay, T. Carl Moore, H. Burke Nicholson, Henry H. Smith, and F. Carter Tate.

The records on their subjects do not seem to be up-to-date.

"I usually talk about Atlanta history," Garrett says.

An unsigned comment on a page of minutes of the Symposium, not dated: "I wonder what these old geezers can find to talk about after 26 years of chatter. . . . "

CHAPTER 15

1961

Irreconcilable Differences

On January 15, 1961, a sad article appeared in the *Atlanta Constitution*, written by William Osborne. It was headlined "WIFE BURNED PAPERS, HISTORIAN GARRETT SAYS." The article followed:

> Franklin M. Garrett, Atlanta historian and director of The Coca-Cola Co.'s office of information, has filed divorce proceedings against his wife because of alleged cruel "treatment" including the burning of approximately 20 envelopes which contained valuable information about the history of Atlanta.
>
> The burning of the envelopes, some of which contained original manuscripts written by Mr. Garrett, occurred in January in the Garretts' residence at 3225 Paces Ferry Rd., N.W., it was charged in the divorce petition on file in the Fulton Superior Court Clerk's office.
>
> Mr. Garrett, 54, who also is chairman of the Fulton County Civil Service Board, began collecting historical items about

Atlanta in 1923, and many of them are said to be "irreplaceable" the petition says.

In the petition Mr. Garrett alleges that his wife "willfully and maliciously destroyed all of the same (the 20 envelopes) completely by burning them in the living room fireplace at the home, said act being utterly without cause or justification. . . ."

When Mr. Garrett discovered the envelopes were missing from his private files in the library at his home, he asked Mrs. Garrett about them, the petition says. Mrs. Garrett, 33, the former Miss Patricia Myhand Abbot of Birmingham, Ala., "denied knowing anything at all about them," said the divorce petition.

Since she had "threatened" on other occasions to burn Mr. Garrett's "valuable records," he began to look for the envelopes, the petition said. The "charred remains" of the papers were found in the living room fireplace.

A hearing has been scheduled for Feb. 20 in the Fulton County Superior Court's Domestic Relations Division to show cause "why prayers of the petition of the plaintiff (Mr. Garrett) should not be granted."

On Jan. 5 Superior Court Judge George P. Whitman, Sr., temporarily enjoined Mrs. Garrett from entering the library at the Garretts' residence and moving the library's contents.

Mr. Garrett's petition said, . . . "He has collected, assembled and classified, from newspapers, periodicals, old photographs, original manuscripts and from various other sources, written material and data concerning the background of Atlanta and its people, a large portion of which is irreplaceable."

He is the author of "*Atlanta and Environs—A Chronicle of Its People and Events.*" He has been active in civic affairs.

Mrs. Garrett is a needlework and clothing designer.

A fact not mentioned in the news revelation: the Garretts had two small children, a daughter, Patricia Abbott Garrett, age eight, and a son, Franklin Miller Garrett, Jr., age five.

Amid the anger, anguish, and irretrievable failure, both parents were committed to the tender care and continued love and protection of the children, a commitment that was never to be broken.

CHAPTER 16

1974

Garrett Publishes Yesterday's Atlanta—
A Pictorial Review

Twenty years after the publication of *Atlanta and Environs*, Garrett's comprehensive chronicle of Atlanta's people and events, he published another and more accessible history of the region.

Using 230 historic photographs from the archives and library of the Atlanta Historical Society, he began with Atlanta's oldest landmark, the Zero Mile Post, a square stone post with the inscription "W. AND A. R.R. #00," dated 1850. Working from that symbolic landmark, Garrett developed an abbreviated narrative of Atlanta's past to accompany a pictorial evocation of the city's kaleidoscope from the days of the Creek Indians in 1852. *Yesterday's Atlanta* was published in Miami, Florida, by E. A. Seeman, Pub., in 1974.

In addition to a crisp and colorful recounting of the events of ten decades, the illustrations were defined by completely descriptive outlines. The captions themselves were small historic notes.

The book was widely read at that time and in 1982, six years later, became the basis of a six-part television documentary that aired over Channel 30 (WPBA) and the Georgia Public Television network.

Garrett himself narrated the miniseries, covering Atlanta-area history from the days of wilderness Terminus to 1952 and "the future apparently which knows no boundaries."

Chris Moser, producer of the documentary for WETV, drew on the Historical Society's library and archives for vintage photographs, sketches, lithographs, documents, and maps relating to the period from the 1820s to the mid-century mark.

The series was Garrett's first major television project, and it took him to many Atlanta locations where he contrasted "what is with what was." Vintage film footage and photographs, illustrations by the late Wilbur G. Kurtz, Sr., and other artifacts and historical reenactments helped to create a visual sense of the city through the years.

According to *Options,* WABE's publication at the time, the production of *Yesterday's Atlanta* was a true civic effort. Many agencies and organizations made their resources available, including Georgia Public Television, the Georgia Department of Archives and History, the DeKalb Historical Society, and seven historians, in addition to Garrett, consulting and taking part in the filming.

A small army of volunteers helped with research, unearthed photographs, performed in reenactments, raised funds, and handled other tasks that helped lighten the loads of producer Chris Moser and director Thomas Joyce. Production costs were reduced thanks to the contributed services of such supporters as Stone Mountain and Kennesaw Mountain Parks, the Victorian Society, Costume Crafters, Wheels Across Atlanta, Westville Historical Handicrafts, and the Atlanta chapter of the American Antique Automobile Club.

The family of the late Mayor William B. Hartsfield made his personal film collection available for use.

The project was financially assisted by the National Endowment for the Humanities through the Georgia Endowment for the Humanities and by contributions from the J. M. Tull Foundation, the Metropolitan Atlanta Community Foundation, Atlanta Gas Light Company, Amoco Oil Company, The Coca-Cola Company, Georgia Power Company, Communication Channels, Southern Bell, the Walter H. and Marjory M. Rich Memorial Fund, Cousins Properties, the Selig Foundation, and Mrs. Ivan Allen, Jr.

It was no small project.

The series has been repeated (at least once since), and "it will be seen again and again."

Continuing from *Options:*

> The history of Atlanta is the captivating story of a city carved out of the wilderness by railroads, devastated by the Civil War, rebuilt out of the ashes, stalled by the Great Depression, chosen in a hard-fought battle to be the aviation center of the South and guided by wise and progressive leaders throughout the turbulent years of Black Americans' struggle for civil rights.
>
> It is the story of remarkable individuals: Henry Grady, Rebecca Latimer Felton, Robert Woodruff, Alonzo Herndon, Margaret Mitchell, and William B. Hartsfield among them.

The back cover of the paper-bound book contained four approving reviews of the original publication:

Atlanta Journal-Constitution: "Garrett's gently witty and thoroughly informed picture captions would be hard to beat anywhere. Garrett provided succinct summary of the highlights of the city's history, but the main delight is the pictures and Garrett's descriptions. It's like having an Atlanta Historical Society on your own bookshelf."

Georgia Life: "Here we find pictures of early public school classes, businesses, homes, street scenes, railroads, prominent personalities, and news events. All in all, a fairly complete fascinating covering of the important aspects of Atlanta's past . . . well worth the price, and it will be a necessary supplement to any future or past history of Atlanta."

Southern Living: "Garrett writes incisive, informative chapters and really lends the book much of its interest and most of its authenticity through his very specific outlines to the photographs."

Georgia Historical Quarterly: "The well-known official historian of Atlanta presents an interesting and balanced book of the Gate City of the South. . . . This is a well done book that should be of great interest to longtime Atlantans or those who want to learn more of her physical past."

Under the headline "Garrett Enlivens Yesterday's Atlanta," Richard Zoglin, then television and radio editor of the *Atlanta Constitution*, writing on November 9, 1982, both criticized and praised the production.

Calling it a major achievement for Channel 30, a perennially underfinanced PBS station, he added that the first program, "which covers the years from 1812 to 1850, is not all one might hope for. Producer Moser's main problem is figuring out what to put on the screen while Garrett is talking. Although he makes good use of vintage pictures, much of the time we're simply watching Garrett himself from an uncomfortable distance, or static shots of street signs and the like."

Added Zoglin:

> The show's most creative solution to this visual dilemma is a series of dramatic reenactments of significant events in Atlanta history . . . early settlers driving a stake in the spot where Terminus (later Marthasville and finally Atlanta) was founded. But these wordless dramatic scenes are stilted and amateurish, like a seventh-grade historical pageant.
>
> Yet Garrett himself is an appealing talker, and he manages to be both conversational and informative. And there's much fascinating material in *Yesterday's Atlanta*, especially when Garrett stresses the links between the city's past and present. He shows us the spot, for instance, where Hardy Ivy built his cabin, the first white man's residence in what is now the city limits. The Marriott Hotel, Garrett points out, now sits on the spot.
>
> . . . The first episode, entitled "Indians Out, White Man In" seems to gloss over any unpleasantness that may have attended that transition.
>
> Still, if *Yesterday's Atlanta* isn't definitive TV history, it certainly makes a valuable contribution. Channel 30 deserves a round of applause for bringing it to us.

CHAPTER 17

1978

Marriage to Frances Steele Finney

arrett had been living for fifteen years as a bachelor when he suddenly decided to call an old colleague at The Coca-Cola Company. Frances Steele Finney's husband had died, and she was living as a widow.
Her only child, Perry Mark Finney, was grown and living in Minneapolis.

"You've never heard me give a talk, have you?" Franklin inquired. "I
have to make one at a black tie affair, and I need a lady to be with me."

She accepted his invitation. She heard him make his talk. Two years
later they were married.

"The best thing I ever did," Franklin has told many friends since that
event. "She was just the perfect one for me."

As for his bride, she was equally enthusiastic about the union. "I love
his work. I respect his achievements, and I enjoy his friends and the necessary routine. We have a busy life, and I couldn't be happier."

They were married at noon, October 14, 1978, in the First Presbyterian
Church with the Rev. Paul T. Eckel and the Rev. John Newton officiat-
ing. The Rev. Newton, a former member of the clergy at Peachtree Presbyterian Church and a cousin of Frances Garrett, shared duties in the ceremony.

In anticipation of their wedding, Garrett, who had been a member of Trinity Presbyterian, had joined First Presbyterian, where Frances had long been a member, on July 23, 1978.

After a wedding dinner at the Piedmont Driving Club, the newly married Garretts boarded the Southern Crescent to New York and there boarded the *S.S. Statendam* for a cruise to Bermuda as a honeymoon.

Franklin M. and Frances Steele Finney Garrett, ca. 1988. Photo courtesy of Franklin M. Garrett

While she may never have heard Garrett make a public address before his fateful invitation to her, Frances Finney had known her new husband better than he realized. She had first accepted a position in the office of public relations, consumer affairs, at Coca-Cola in 1956 and within a short period of time had been transferred to the office of information, which Garrett then headed.

When Franklin Garrett retired in 1968, Frances joined the legal department, trademark division, headed by Julius Lunsford. In 1972, she was asked to join the Coca-Cola export division to assist in its move from New York to Atlanta. She took retirement from Coke in 1978 after twenty-two years with the company. The Garretts were married that year.

After their honeymoon, the Garretts returned to Roxboro Road to set up housekeeping together. The house, of course, was the first "Mainline," overlooking the Southern Railway tracks, which were a great part of the location's attraction to Garrett. He loved to see the trains go by, as did his guests.

Frances was accomplished in her own right. After graduating from Agnes Scott College in 1937 with a B.A. in sociology and economics, she had spent two years as an area supervisor for the National Youth Administration and eight years with the southeastern region division of the DuPont Company.

While a student at Agnes Scott College, she was president of the Glee Club, member of the Blackfriars Dramatic Club, an avid tennis player, co-winner of the doubles matches, and member of the May court.

President of her class and its fund chair, she has been unflagging in her devotion to the college. She has been a member of the Agnes Scott College alumnae board since 1981 and has served in many capacities as an alumna. In 1990, her service as chair of the acquisitions committee won her the Outstanding Alumna Award for service to the college.

Forced to move from their Roxboro home by the development of MARTA (Metropolitan Atlanta Rapid Transit Authority), which required their space, the Garretts planned a new home on Randall Mill Road to accommodate their needs and provide suitable space for Franklin's library and his collection of railroad memorabilia.

Their new house, a stunning one-story design with two separate wings connected by a long and spacious hall, has attracted the attention of several national home magazines, including *Southern Homes* in 1988.

With glowing photographs by Bard Wrisley, Lynn Burnett McGill, managing editor of *Southern Homes*, defined the new "Mainline" as a sophisticated city version of a nineteenth-century small plantation house, especially noting its beautiful Clarence House wallpaper and its general air of cheer.

"It is not often that lifetimes of accumulations fit together so well," Ms. McGill wrote. "The belongings of each blends easily into a cohesive whole and the Garretts were able to put it all in special display areas throughout the house."

"He had porcelain, I had cut glass," *Southern Homes* quoted Frances as saying. "So niches were made for the former, while the latter was housed in a breakfront in the parlor."

"In the end," wrote Lynn McGill, "it is the mellow spirit of the Garretts that pervades this house and lends it warmth and wit. Their graceful approach to life and friends embodied by their living space is truly what their beloved city is all about."

Sadly, Mrs. Garrett's son, Perry Mark Finney, died in 1986 in Minneapolis, where he lived with his wife and three children. He died after a long bout with lymphoma.

The Garretts live a busy civic and social schedule. She is a member of the DAR, Cherokee chapter; the National Society of Colonial Dames of America, Atlanta Township; and the National Society of Magna Carta Dames. She is also welcomed and urged to attend the many groups that have been a part of Garrett's lifetime.

Garrett belongs to the Atlanta Civil War Round Table, the Atlanta Art Association, the Piedmont Driving Club, and the Commerce Club. He is a member of Kappa Phi Kappa, the professional education fraternity; the Intercollegiate Law Fraternity of Sigma Delta Kappa; the National Railway Historical Society; the Symposium; the Georgia Genealogical Society; the Rotary Club of Atlanta; Omicron Delta Kappa, the honorary leadership society; and the English Speaking Union. In May 1970, Mr. Garrett received an honorary degree, doctor of humane letters, from Oglethorpe College.

Garrett is past president and has held almost all the other offices of the Atlanta Historical Society. He is a member of the Georgia Historical Society; the DeKalb Historical Society; the South Carolina Historical Society; the American Legion, Post 134; the Newcomen Society of North America; a former member of the board of directors, Children's Center of Metropolitan Atlanta, Inc.; former chairman of the Fulton County Personnel Board; past president of the Grand Jurors Association of Fulton County; and former member of the Atlanta Civic Design Commission. He has been a member of the Atlanta Landmarks Board of the historic Fox Theatre since it was formed in 1978 to raise desperately needed funds to save it from destruction.

——— — ———

A jaunty couple, dressed for a late dinner at the Cherokee Club, arrived at the valet exit. "My Stutz Bearcat '24,' the man ordered, straight-faced. The attendant scurried away to return promptly with a four-door red Oldsmobile. "I brought your Red Rocket instead, Mr. Garrett," the young man said. "It was parked closer." On the back bumper of the Red Rocket was a sassy sticker: "My Other Car Is a Locomotive."

——— — ———

Hal and Mary Louise Clarke, who for many years have had another home in Thomastown, in Kilkenny, Ireland, invited the Garretts to visit them there. Kilkenny had a very active historical society and the Clarkes thought it would be a good idea for Garrett to speak to them, tell them what a real society should be, and how to raise money. He made a delightful talk and suggestions, and they were all charmed by him.

Mary Louise then took up the story: "There was another special fall-out from their visit. Many years ago we learned that the Candler family came from a town called Callan, in County Kilkenny, and through a very interesting situation . . .

"A young man named Candler fell in love with an Irish girl. He, of course, was a Protestant, she a Catholic. They were married, but later every record of their marriage was stricken from the records.

"The Kilkenny Society had tried for many years to make the connection with the Candler family and had not been able to manage it.

"So I talked to Franklin about it and when he got back to Atlanta he found a copy of Charles Howard Candler's history of the Candler family. I then gave that to the local historical society, and they did make the connection. Incidentally, The Coca-Cola Company sponsored the party. . . ."

——— — ———

On Tuesday, March 5, 1991, "Peach Buzz," in the *Atlanta Constitution*, opened its column with the announcement that Atlanta historian Franklin Garrett "defends his title at the All Men's Flower-Arranging Competition, which kicks off the Atlanta Flower Show on Wednesday at the Apparel Mart. Challengers include DeKalb commish Hosea Williams, the Alliance Theatre's Kenny Leon, WGST's Ralph from Ben Hill, Zoo Atlanta's Terry Maple, artist Comer Jennings, and the new Botanical Garden director Robert Bowden. Last year, Garrett won with simplicity. 'I took two long-stemmed flowers, adjusted them at a suitable angle and won.' 'What kind of flowers?' 'I have no idea,' he said with a laugh.

A letter dated March 7 from Lisa Frank, public relations manager of the Atlanta Botanical Garden, thanked Franklin: "On behalf of everyone at the Atlanta Botanical Garden, thanks a million for sharing your time and talents at the All Men's Flower-Arranging Competition. Once again, you put your heart and soul into it.

"Keep up your good work."

——— — ———

Franklin Garrett was a man of many surprises, including a memory with almost total recall and a spirit to match. Seen anywhere within a radius of thirty miles in metropolitan Atlanta, on a platform, with or without a microphone, in a remote or renowned cemetery, on some special home-coming day, or even on an ancient railroad trestle, audiences never knew what to expect from him.

Nor, necessarily, did he. For years he has not bothered to lecture, if he ever had. He just remembered.

For instance, he was requested one day by his confident wife, Frances, to fill in at a moment's notice at a women's study group when the regular reviewer had failed to show. Garrett stood and reflected: "Well, since neither you nor I have any notes, I think I will just review Oswald Spengler's *Decline of the West.*"

Laughter, uneasy laughter.

Garrett, being himself, might just take on Spengler. And they all had luncheon or bridge dates later.

Garrett relieved his friends by talking a brisk fifteen minutes about the 1930s and their old golfing friend, Bobby Jones, and the Atlanta sportswriter who wrote best about him, O. B. Keeler. The ladies, who knew both Jones and Keeler, listened raptly as if it were all new and fresh to them.

They appreciated that Garrett knew Atlanta and its citizens, past and present, by heart. The community had been his inner domain and under his literal scrutiny for longer and more intimately than anybody then extant.

CHAPTER 18

Corporate Histories, Forewords, Etc.

Hardly a year has passed since the 1950s that Garrett has not been the author of some history of importance to a specific portion of the community.

Before *Atlanta and Environs* had made its appearance in 1954, he had completed a detailed account of the Trust Company of Georgia in 1948, the Young Men's Christian Association in 1952, and, in 1954, the history of the Federal Reserve Bank in Atlanta.

Others followed: Piedmont Driving Club, 1956; J. M. Tull Company, 1957; Adair Realty and Loan Company, 1965; The Coca-Cola Company, 1974; Atlanta Historical Society, 1979; Peachtree Golf Club, 1979; Westview Cemetery, 1987.

In 1962, William Bailey Williford, an Atlanta public relations man whose avocations were history and writing, brought out a book called *Peachtree Street, Atlanta* published by the University of Georgia Press. The book described the evolution of Atlanta from an Indian trail in the 1840s to its rebuilding after the 1860s on to its present skyline.

Williford acknowledged the assistance he received from the Georgia State Library, the Department of Archives and History, the Atlanta Historical Society, the Atlanta Public Library, and the Ida Dunlap Little Memorial Library, and "special thanks go to Franklin M. Garrett for his personal assistance and for the invaluable aid received from his definitive *Atlanta and Environs*."

In 1978, Harold H. Martin expressed his gratitude to William L. Pressly and Franklin Garrett of the Atlanta Historical Society for conceiving and sponsoring his new book *The First Hundred Years: The Life*

Franklin M. Garrett with one of his publications, 1956. Photo courtesy of the Atlanta History Center

and Work of Mayor William B. Hartsfield, "including, of course, that infallible source, Mr. Garrett's own book *Atlanta and Environs*."

In 1983, Norman Shavin and Bruce Galphin brought out *Atlanta: Triumph of a People, An Illustrated History*, with a graceful introduction by Franklin M. Garrett, historian, Atlanta Historical Society. In their own acknowledgments, Shavin and Galphin wrote: "Garrett's role was essential. Not only was his two-volume *Atlanta and Environs* an absolute gold mine, as many writers of Atlanta history know, but he also read this entire history text, made important suggestions, saved us from embarrassing errors and wrote the introduction." Shavin is now deceased, but Galphin has expressed his appreciation of Garrett: "He is astonishing. His entire career has been a veritable mental magnet, attracting all information and every fact. And he is so generous with it all. We could not have done *Triumph of a People* without him. . . ."

In 1987, the Atlanta Historical Society published the fourth volume of *Atlanta and Environs*, this one written by Harold H. Martin. Martin, a longtime journalist and much-admired writer, was especially chosen by Garrett to bring up-to-date Garrett's earlier volumes of *Atlanta and Environs*. The three early volumes had ended with the 1930s and the new volume was to cover the 1940s to the 1970s. Garrett had obtained funding to finance Martin's work.

But all did not go as smoothly as expected. Martin became seriously ill during the preparation of his assignment and expressed his anxiety and appreciation to Garrett in many notes and references: "To my favorite historian, Franklin Garrett, who asked me to do the fourth volume of his famous history of *Atlanta and Environs*. This is it . . . and the last of a long-hand epic I will ever attempt. With gratitude to him and the University of Georgia Press." It was signed, shakily, Harold Martin.

A poignant handwritten note dated February 25, 1988: "Franklin, I want to put in writing my truly deep appreciation of your friendship and the inspiration you have been to me during these recent years . . . when my failing memory . . . though not my physical bodily condition have made life very difficult for me. Sincerely your friend, Harold Martin."

The final book was severely shortened, and Bradley R. Rice, editor of *Atlanta History*, the journal of the Atlanta Historical Society, gave credit to Lil Salter, who also assisted Martin and typed the original manuscript for the fourth volume of *Atlanta and Environs.*

In 1991, Garrett wrote a long foreword to a large book entitled *The Capital City Club—The First One Hundred Years* by James C. Bryant, Ph.D. The foreword was headed with a large portrait of Garrett and concluded: "All in all this centennial history will make a significant contribution to the social and cultural heritage of Atlanta, and at the same time provide the club membership with a lasting source of pride and satisfaction."

Most recently, Franklin has added his approving imprimatur to a foreword to a new history of Buckhead, *Account of the North Side,* by Susan K. Barnard.

His comment: "The result is both informative and highly readable. Indeed, a welcome addition to the literature of an important and colorful part of Georgia."

——— — ———

As the owner of all Atlanta city directories, Garrett was often called upon to make statistical reports before public bodies in Georgia.

In August 1959, Mike Edwards, then a reporter for the *Atlanta Journal* and now associate editor of *National Geographic* magazine, reported that Franklin Garrett had told the Metropolitan Planning Commission that in the Atlanta of 1860, population 7,741, the federal census showed the city had 23 barkeepers, 1 distiller, 3 gamblers, 49 prostitutes, 9 slave traders, 1 man described as an "old loafer." Also 12 clergymen, 20 teachers, and 1 person described as a "young lady."

Also 9 grass widows, 1 man "at rest," 1 man "at rest for a year," and 5 persons in jail. Also 41 lawyers, 1 freight engineer, 188 people, 2 bankers, and 2 shavers (persons who lent money), 1 architect, 41 doctors, 9 dentists, 235 carpenters and 48 brick masons, 59 locomotive engineers and 66 locomotive firemen.

——— — ———

CHAPTER 19

1980

"Papa Loves the Railroad So Much"

On April 8, 1980, the Georgia Railroad gave Franklin Garrett what every normal boy wants when he is seventy-three years old—his own diesel locomotive to play with for a whole day, with his name blazing on the side, and his own number, 6051.

Garrett's wife, Frances, smashed a bottle of champagne on the locomotive's robust flank, a Dixieland band jazzed happily, and 150 or so train buff friends, governors, mayors, politicians, and financiers cheered incredulously as Engineer Garrett took the controls to go forth to guide Train 108 "on its maiden run, a mile or two down the line in the direction of Montgomery and back." Another account mentioned Social Circle, Georgia, as the destination.

No matter the destination, that day Train 108 was powered by engine SBD 6051-6805-6653 and 1638 and consisted of thirty box cars, two coaches, and one caboose, and the coaches were occupied by fifty passengers.

Standing with the well-wishers near the Foundry Street entrance to the World Congress Center, Garrett's son, Miller, then twenty-three, declared this the greatest thing that could have happened to his father, the great-

"Engineer" Franklin M. Garrett prepares to operate his locomotive, Georgia Railroad's No. 6051, April 1980. Photo courtesy of the Atlanta History Center

est honor that anyone could have bestowed.

"Papa just loves the railroad so much," his son said. "Always has, so much."

Practically every feature writer and commentator in the area has found Garrett and his adventures endlessly fascinating. The afternoon paper, the *Atlanta Journal*, rushed to the presses to get a six-column photo of city historian Franklin Garrett waving to the crowd after "his" locomotive was christened.

The next morning, Elmo Ellis, WSB Radio's general manager, broadcast the news

> The ceremonies were bright and colorful and took place right on the railroad tracks, adjacent to the World Congress Center. . . . Many of our town's best personalities were on hand to attend the splendid luncheon and then voice their approval.

The special event was engineered by M. S. Jones, Jr., the president and general manager of the Georgia Railroad. He and some of his colleagues thought it would be a very appropriate thing to name a locomotive for a man who not only loves trains, but probably knows as much about them as anybody in this country.

That's not all Franklin Garrett knows. He also happens to be Atlanta's foremost authority on the history of this city and its people. Years ago he did a monumental research in compiling and writing *Atlanta and Environs*, the ultimate authority on the origin and development of our town. Naming a brand-new diesel in Franklin Garrett's honor is one splendid way to show him that we appreciate him. But actually the people of Atlanta owe this fine man much more than this. He is the one individual, above all, in my mind, who gives Atlanta a sense of continuity, tying our past with the present and the future.

And thanks to his dedicated efforts to capture and preserve the best of our past, he has helped immeasurably to give us a sense of direction as we move toward a brighter tomorrow.

The gamesmanship between Garrett, "locomotive engineer," and others in the Seaboard System Railroad continued until they had wrung the last posture from it.

On May 2, 1981, C. E. Gilpin, road foreman of engineers, wrote "To those Concerned: Regarding Garrett's instruction in proper train handling." Gilpin allowed that it was his considered opinion that as a result of having been instructed in proper train handling between Stone Mountain, Georgia, and Lithonia, Georgia, by locomotive engineer W. S. Mauldin, Sr., and with Gilpin's own presence on that date as a participant, he was ready to attest that should the need arise, Mr. Franklin Garrett could be called upon to run trains between Stone Mountain and Lithonia, Georgia, on the Georgia Railroad.

To which Garrett, "locomotive engineer," replied with sincere thanks for the notification. "While I am eminently qualified as to throttle and whistle, I must say that my expertise with train and engine air brakes needs beefing up.

"At any rate, I am proud to be a Georgia Railroad Locomotive Engineer, and this appointment illustrates the old truism that it is never too late in life to start a new career.

"I would appreciate it if you would transmit a copy of this letter to W. S. Mauldin, Sr., who, in my mind, epitomizes the typical locomotive engineer with all the character and reliability that goes with such a position.

"I would like to follow up his suggestion that the AAR somehow recognize the Georgia Railroad for its long safety record in operating a mixed train. If you can tell me with whom to correspond, I shall be glad to follow up the suggestion."

The *Atlanta Journal* noted that Garrett was the first to have had a locomotive named for him since 1890.

Which, of course, gave Garrett an opportunity to do some reminiscing about the past. "The Central of Georgia set the railroad world and the traveling public agog in 1893 when it put the Nancy Hanks in service between Atlanta and Savannah. (This train was not named for Abe Lincoln's mother, but for the swiftest trotting horse in the world at that time, which set a record of 2:04 for the mile at Terre Haute, Indiana, in 1892.)

"The train was elaborate and luxurious and was painted a royal blue from pilot to rear marker lights and was trimmed in gold leaf. A likeness of the horse was blown into the frosted-glass panel above each window of the coaches.

"The engine crew of the Nancy Hanks were furnished with leather caps, painted blue, with gold stripes around them. Nancy Hanks was painted just above the bill. Conductors were distinguished by white vests adorned with pearl buttons, and invariably tipped their caps when lifting tickets from lady passengers.

"The speed of the Nancy was epitomized in an old railroad ditty:

> Some folks say that the Nancy can't run
> But stop, let me tell you what the Nancy done—
> She left Atlanta at half past one
> And got to Savannah at the settin' of the sun,

The Nancy run so fast,
She burnt the wind and scorched the grass.

"The running time of the Nancy was six hours, which was too fast
for the light rails of the period. Old-timers equipped with elastic imagi-
nations tell of the time the Nancy hit a wagonload of corn on a grade
crossing. The sky was full of corn, and it went so high it sprouted before
coming back to earth.

"On August 13, 1893, after nearly seven months of speed and excitement, the Nancy Hanks was taken off the rails."

——— — ———

Garrett has a natural bent toward architecture and antique furniture and
has been successful in combining them with the allure of railroads and
trains. In February of 1975, when he was living as a bachelor at 3434
Roxboro Road, N.E., overlooking the Southern Railroad's Main Lines,
the very selective house tour committee of Egleston Hospital's fund-
raising leadership chose Garrett's first "Mainline" as one of the features
of its spring tour.

Listing the residence in *Garden Gateways*, the official bulletin of the
Garden Club of Georgia, Garrett's house was described as having "antique
furnishings, reminiscent fine oil paintings and a general design providing a gracious environment for one of the finest historical book collections in the nation, including voluminous records of America's railroads.

"The owner is a chronicler of Atlanta's past, and one room off the pan-
eled upstairs library is devoted to records being used for his next book.
Railroad tracks bound the grounds to the rear, and the house is affectionately called 'Mainline.'"

Explaining his agreement to open his home for the annual Egleston
Home and Garden Tour, Garrett apologized that while his home was not
quite completed, he nonetheless enjoyed having friends in late for drinks
and hors d'oeuvres before dining at his club.

Yolande Gwin, *Atlanta Journal* society editor, wrote that "the ingre-
dients of Mainline are plentiful but conversation is the main dish. All of
Mr. Garrett's guests share his interest in history and trains. Wherever they

gather in his two-story home, somewhat of a literary atmosphere is evident amid the furnishings of 18th century style." ·

Miss Gwin continued: "Mr. Garrett has had his finger on the historical pulse of Atlanta for years, and he can entertain his guests with stories with the same fascination, intrigue and mystery as Scheherazade in *A Thousand and One Nights.*

"He can enthrall guests for hours telling about certain phases of Atlanta history, especially if they are newcomers to the city. Women guests, who never think about a train unless it's for a trip, sit for hours examining Mr. Garrett's collection of model trains. Guests can entertain themselves too by turning back the pages of history as they pore through such valuable books as city directories.

"What other host could provide such things as New York's first directory printed in 1789? Or some from Chicago before the great fire, as well as the first one printed in Cincinnati, Washington and the only one printed in Atlanta before the War Between the States? Think now, who could do this?

"Conversation is served with many flavors to whet the appetite of all guests, but there is another form of entertainment which Mr. Garrett's guests enjoy.

"THEY CAN WATCH THE TRAINS GO BY!

"It is almost like a cue for a stage play. Guests gathered at Mr. Garrett's on any evening may be sipping and nibbling. About 8:45 P.M. a shrill whistle pierces the still of the night.

"There is a mad dash for the slate-floored back terrace, or the second-story porch.

"'There she comes!' shouts Mr. Garrett, of course referring to the Southern Railroad's northbound train.

"Naturally, everybody remembers to wave at the passing train as she roars northward.

"Guests don't have much time to settle down to talking again, before Mr. Garrett, as if by magic, says:

"'We'll go back to the porch about 9 o'clock.'

"So about 9 o'clock here comes another train around the bend, her whistles blowing. It is a special train with truck trailers riding piggyback. It rushes by with lightning-like speed.

"'It's real entertainment every evening,' says Mr. Garrett."

Miss Gwin missed one part of the evening well remembered by other guests. One of the special moments came when all the guests had cocktails in their hands. They were led to the proper position on the porch or balcony. On signal, they raised their libations in salute to the passing train. If all went well, the conductor or the engineer saw this little tribute and waved or tipped his cap to the party.

"It kind of made the evening," said one guest who had often tipped a glass to Garrett's passing trains.

Garrett has had a way of including amusing incidents in his serious essays and articles. He has been a dedicated proponent of railroads all his life and believes they were the greatest asset any economy could hope for.

——— — ———

On July 31, 1988, Martha Woodham, writing in the *Atlanta Constitution*, told that Franklin Garrett appeared on all three networks during convention week when he was trapped in an elevator at the Peachtree Plaza Hotel. While they were awaiting an elevator repairman from Lawrenceville, Garrett serenaded the other elevator captives with a few ditties—hits such as "The Frozen Logger" and some railroad laments.

Privately, he has referred loyally to trains and their charms at every opportunity. His last two homes have borne the name "Mainline" on his mailbox and personal letterheads. His office and residences have been embellished with memorabilia of the glories of the rails, and when his last home was designed, architect Clement Ford provided a ledge track down a long front hall for a model of the Southern Crescent train to rest comfortably.

When MARTA was being voted on by the electorate, he was fervent in his approval.

"It failed the first time, but I voted for it again. I use it every time I can."

He has also been a staunch advocate for a multimodal station for downtown Atlanta. "North Carolina and Florida are both in the high-speed rail project, but Georgia . . . a state that built its economy on transportation, is noticeable by its absence."

CHAPTER 20

Applause . . . Applause

Tributes

Along the way, Garrett's companions and colleagues have always warmly applauded his dazzling work.

On Garrett's eightieth birthday, on behalf of the editors of the area and the trustees of the Atlanta Historical Society, Jack Spalding, president, wrote:

> Dear Franklin:
>
> Today we celebrate your birthday and also the fact that you and the Atlanta Historical Society are inseparable.
>
> That you are somewhat older than the Society is fitting for in many respects you have been the parent and the Society the child.
>
> You were there in its infancy and at one point you lived with it in order to protect it from intruders and those who might have wished to profane its relics. You have saved it from error. *Atlanta and Environs* is the unimpeachable source.
>
> The history of our city now is fact rather than legend, thanks to you. That this history is so well known is because you have been eager to teach it. The number of grounds and organizations you have instructed is large. The number of stu-

dents, writers, reporters and just curious whose questions you patiently have answered is staggering.

Your devotion to the Society is magnificent, your loyalty unbeatable and your knowledge profound.

The business of this Society is the history of Atlanta and while it has other ramifications now, when all is said and done these ramifications only adorn this repository of fact which you in great part have collected, collated and promulgated.

There is no end to the work of historians. Atlanta is young and many centuries of her history, perhaps, are still to be written. May we and our successors continue to build on your foundations, preserving our history, free of error, myth and distortion. With admiration and great affection . . . .

Jack Spalding
For the Trustees

——— — ———

Another letter, on behalf of advertising and public relations professionals, from George Goodwin, for Manning, Selvage and Lee/Atlanta:

Dear Franklin:

It is Tuesday. I need to know the population of Atlanta in 1888, and you are in Europe. What is a fellow to do? This true-life situation that boiled up this morning reminds me again how valuable you are and how bereft our town would be without you. Other sources might provide the census figures for 1880 and 1890, but only you could tell me why the population jumped nearly 100 percent.

All of which brings me to the point of congratulating you on your 80th birthday and at the same time insisting that you stay handy. You are a wonderful citizen of our town; we could not get along without you.

Sincerely,
George Goodwin

——— — ———

From J. W. Jones, senior vice president (retired), The Coca-Cola Company:

Dear Franklin:

Upon reaching the age of four score and ten, the late Mr. James Cash Penney published his "Views from the Ninth Decade." I trust you will consider beginning preparation of a similar tome to be followed by a supplemental treatise dealing with the tenth decade. This is by way of affirming my conviction that you are one of those individuals who appear indestructible, and all of us are thereby the beneficiaries. Your service to The Coca-Cola system, to the Atlanta Historical Society and to the social and business community of Atlanta is noteworthy for its effectiveness and all of us are grateful.

We salute you on this 80th anniversary of your birthday.

Cordially yours,

Joe

——— — ———

From Roberto C. Goizueta, chairman of the board and chief executive officer, The Coca-Cola Company:

Dear Franklin:

I am delighted to send this greeting from your many friends and associates of The Coca-Cola Company on the occasion of your 80th birthday. Through your career you have ensured future generations of having a more complete historical record for study and you may be proud of your legacy.

To salute you on this milestone, my colleagues and I offer a Coca-Cola toast wishing you all the best for this birthday and many more. And Olguita joins me in sending Frances and you our warmest regards.

Sincerely,

Roberto

——— — ———

For the city of Atlanta, Andrew Young, mayor, wrote:

Dear Mr. Garrett:

I am pleased to join with other well-wishers in congratulating you on the occasion of your 80th birthday.

Your wealth of knowledge about Atlanta's historical development coupled with your contributions to the building and shaping of our society have made you a valuable asset to the Atlanta community.

On behalf of the people of Atlanta, I commend you for reaching this important milestone in your life and wish you many more years of happiness.

Sincerely,
Andrew Young

——— — ———

For the Supreme Court of Georgia, Charles Longstreet Weltner, justice, wrote:

Dear Mr. Ott [then executive director, the Atlanta Historical Society]:

I am hard pressed to put down within the four corners of a piece of paper appropriate sentiments concerning my friend Franklin Garrett.

It has been my pleasure to sit at his feet for the past few years as a member of the Atlanta Symposium, which he serves as Chairman. This is a small group of men who have been meeting (they and their predecessors) monthly since 1905. Franklin is called upon regularly to present matters of interest to the membership, and it is there that I have come to know his wit, his sagacity and his unbelievable breadth of knowledge.

The Atlanta community at large is the great beneficiary of Franklin's restless and ever-broadening search of the great events and small details of our past—all of which serve to illuminate our own time. I am pleased to be included among his friends who have known and worked with him over the years.

Sincerely,

Charles L. Weltner

———— — ————

For the First Presbyterian Church, Paul T. Eckel:

When I look out on a Sunday morning and see you and your lovely wife Frances sitting there on the right side of the church with one of the brightest faces and most responsive in all the congregation, I marvel at the news that you are eighty years old.

It has been an honor to have you as one of our most regular and supportive members. Your encouragement has been rewarding to me and others in your church. Your contributions of lectures, talks and even songs have been the delight of every one of us who shared in them.

In addition to all the ways by which we Atlantans may pay tribute to your prowess as a historian, let me add to that my expression of appreciation for your commitment as a churchman. You have been an example to all who have known you of faithfulness, consistency and discipline. Your brilliance, I might add, is exceeded only by your good sense of humor.

It is an honor for me on behalf of the Session, congregation and Trustees of First Presbyterian Church to offer our heartfelt tribute to you in the celebration of this important day in your life, and special occasion for the Atlanta community.

Your pastor,

Paul T. Eckel

———— — ————

From his lifelong friend, Ivan Allen, Jr., former mayor of Atlanta:

My dearest Franklin:

May we, Louise and I, express our grateful appreciation for

your friendship and contributions to the Atlanta Historical Society on the occasion of your 80th birthday. You have had a wonderful career, and it is deeply appreciated by thousands of Atlantans. You have been the strongest link between the history of the past and present-day occurrence.

We have had the great pleasure of enjoying your friendship during these years, and have marveled at your unequaled capacity of knowledge of the Atlanta scene.

It is most fitting that we have on this occasion of your 80th birthday to express our appreciation of your friendship and contributions.

With appreciation and affection, I am,
Sincerely yours,
Ivan Allen, Jr.

——— — ———

From Julian S. Carr, attorney at law, the blithest of tributes:

Dear Franklin:
Kill the fatted calf, sound the gong, fire the heavy artillery, salute eighty guns, ring the railroad whistle and bring on the welcome knell of the birthday bell . . . for that

elevated, cultivated, educated, celebrated
nobleman, Franklin the Garrett!

Congratulations from us and all of our family.
Anne and I admire and cherish you.

Sincerely yours,
Julian S. Carr

——— — ———

From James A. Mackay, president, DeKalb Historical Society:

Dear Franklin:
On behalf of the DeKalb Historical Society, I extend our congratulations to you on your 80th birthday. If anyone in the city of Atlanta appears to me to be indispensable, I think that it is you.

Our Society prides itself in the fact that you are a charter member, and that you have consistently supported and aided us from year to year. We particularly appreciate the fact that your scholarship has provided the best history of DeKalb County to date. We lean totally on your work to know about our history from the founding of the county until 1852 and much of the rest of your scholarship aids us in understanding DeKalb County in its relationship to the metropolitan area.

I want to add my own personal expression of appreciation for the pleasure it has been for me to be your colleague in the Symposium. Those evenings have been among the richest in my whole life, and I always remember with special pleasure your papers and your hospitality in your own home.

There is so much more to say, but for now I wish you many more productive years and God's richest blessings for you and your lovely wife.

Sincerely yours,
Jamie

——— — ———

From Judson C. Ward, Jr., Ph.D., dean of Emory University Alumni:

Dear Franklin:

. . . Although I had high regard for you before I spent two years at the Atlanta Historical Society, I developed even greater respect and regard for you and what you mean to Atlanta. I came to know that it will take a staff of ten or twelve researchers to answer all the questions that come to the Society once you are gone. Now you answer them *ex tempore* over the telephone without even referring to books or documents. Your knowledge and memory are phenomenal for a man of fifty much less eighty. Keep answering those letters and callers and keep stumping the Young Historians.

As you know, no one else will ever have the opportunity or desire to spend virtually all his life delving into Atlanta history. In that sense you are truly unique . . . a resource that cannot and will not be replaced. I join the hundreds who admire you and appreciate all that you mean to the preservation of our heritage . . . .

Sue joins me in sending our very best to you and Frances.

Sincerely yours,

Jake

———— — ————

From William L. Pressly, founder and president emeritus of the Westminster Schools:

How happy I am with the place you have made for yourself at the Society and among the people of Atlanta. Your speeches are scintillating and informative. Your store of historical materials which you recall instantly is astonishing. Your courtesy, friendliness and thoughtfulness are so innate that you are the close friend of innumerable people . . . they all know they can count on you.

As historian of the Atlanta Historical Society, you are superb. As Necrologist you are accomplishing a monumental task which will serve generations of Atlantans. . . .

Give my love to Frances,

Cordially,

Bill

———— — ————

From Ann Woodall, a coworker at the Atlanta History Center:

Dear Mr. Garrett:
                    Church bells will resound,
                    Train whistles will sing out
                    Coca-Cola will fizz,
                    Citizens will cheer at each corner
                    of the original Land Lots, and no one will
                    call to inquire where Tara is . . .

Indeed, all of Atlanta's institutions will be saluting this man who has memorialized them with verve and veracity for at least seven of those eight decades.

Henry Grady and his associates may get credit for raising a brave and beautiful city, but no one has illuminated its legacy more knowledgeably or lovingly than you. Thank you!

May this day be particularly joyous. John joins me in sending love and heartiest congratulations.

Fondly,
Ann Woodall

——— — ———

HAPPY BIRTHDAY, FRANKLIN GARRETT, OR: TWENTY- THREE LINES (163 WORDS) ON THE SUBJECT OF TURNING EIGHTY.

His legendary mind holds facts of every kind,
And his "environs" are the greatest.
Necrology he's got and stump him we cannot,
His history is the latest.

He would rather take a train than fly an aeroplane,
A locomotive bears his name:
He lives on the Main Line, has the answer every time
And his toasts have brought him fame.

Much more can be told of this sterling and gold
    Personality,
We wish him more than just these first four-score
Years of prosperity.

From,
Lisa Reynolds Hammett
Madison-Morgan Cultural Center, Madison, Georgia

——— — ———

From Tom Watson Brown:

. . . And so I salute you as the official and consummate historian of Atlanta and its environs, dedicated promoter of railway travel, adviser to journalists, politicians, genealogists and amateur historians, gracious host, staunch friend, raconteur, bon vivant, possessor of perennially good humor, author, necrologist, speaker of stentorian tones and, above all, denying the geographical accident of your birth, a true Southern gentleman.

Many more happy returns,

Your friend,
Tom

P.S. My son Durham celebrated his sixth birthday by following your advice and completing *Gibbon's Decline and Fall of the Roman Empire*. What should he master next? Homer? Thucydides? Parkman?

Garrett's note: "Thucydides, Tom, of course. . . ."

——— — ———

Letter from Mrs. A. Dixon (Vee) Adair:

Dear Franklin:

I'll bet my admiration goes back farther than most anyone's—as I was that skinny little five-year-old across the street who used to beg your sister Esther to let me have a peek into Franklin's room, which was lined, all four walls, floor to ceiling, with books. What awe I felt! Could anybody be that smart?

I admired you from afar then, and happily at much closer range now.

Dick joins me in wishing you the happiest of birthdays . . . and in saying how much we cherish you and Frances' friendship.

Vee

1991

Memories of Margaret Mitchell and Saving the Place She Called "The Dump"

On September 22, 1991, the marquee of the treasured Fox Theatre read "AMC THEATRES PRESENTS A SPECIAL SHOWING OF 'GONE WITH THE WIND' HONORING FRANKLIN GARRETT."

Inside the theater that Sunday afternoon were three thousand friends of Franklin who had gathered to contribute generously to the restoration of the house where Margaret Mitchell Marsh had lived with her husband from 1925 to 1932 while she was writing *Gone with the Wind*. In the slang of the toddlin' twenties, the Marshes flippantly called their first apartment "The Dump."

But when it was built in 1895 as a single-family home on Peachtree Street, it was home to some of Atlanta's most important families. Later converted into an apartment building in 1919 and moved to the back of the large lot to face Crescent Avenue, it had continued for years as a respectable residence for dwellers in what is now called Midtown.

However, by 1987, long empty, tattered, and desolate, it was facing demolition when Franklin Garrett turned his attention to it and remarked that its restoration "may be just about our last chance to honor Margaret Mitchell."

Led by Mary Rose Taylor, a trustee of the Atlanta Historical Society and commissioner of the City of Atlanta/Fulton County Recreation Authority, as chair, eleven preservation-minded Atlanta men and women undertook to save "The Dump."

The board members included Eileen Brown, former executive director of the Atlanta Preservation Center; Xernona Clayton, vice president, Turner Broadcasting System, Inc.; Carol Mumford, executive director of the Wren's Nest; and Weston Sprigg, representing the management of Nissan Motor Company, USA. And most touched and pleased, Lillian Clarke, cousin to Margaret Mitchell and former historian of the Junior League of Atlanta.

With a host committee of fifty-six men and women representing every activist preservation group, (including Mr. and Mrs. Eugene Mitchell and Mr. Joseph Mitchell, the family of Margaret Mitchell, the Atlanta Chamber of Commerce, and the Japan-America Society), the benefit was led by the Hon. Maynard Jackson and Mrs. Jackson and three other living mayors and their wives—the Hon. Andrew Young and Mrs. Young, the Hon. and Mrs. Sam Massell, and the Hon. and Mrs. Ivan Allen, Jr.—all interested in bringing the Margaret Mitchell House back to respectability.

Valerie Jackson, the mayor's handsome wife, had awaited the arrival of the Garretts and had swept them forward to the stage of the Fox—which had long been the stage for Atlanta's Metropolitan Opera and other momentous performances—to her husband, Mayor Jackson, who was twice elected.

With welcoming remarks, Mayor Jackson reminded the assemblage that this occasion honored city historian Garrett on the event of his eighty-fifth birthday: "Through his work with the Atlanta History Center and his publication *Atlanta and Environs*, Franklin Garrett not only has been instrumental in preserving our city's past, but he has also been a vital source in helping to shape its future."

A gold-embossed hard-bound program with the words "Franklin, My Dear, . . . We Do Give a Damn," was handed to each guest, compliments of the AMC Theatres.

The program that followed was deserving of Hollywood: television anchors Jocelyn Dorsey and John Pruitt; a birthday tribute written by Tom Watson Brown, produced by O'Connor Burnham and Company; Atlanta's celebrated tenor Sam Hagan singing "Happy Birthday," all in association with Staging Techniques and the Fox Theatre.

But that was not all. An original docudrama, *It May Not Be Tara*, written, directed, and produced by Don Smith of Visibility Communications, presented the raison d'être behind the restoration of the Margaret Mitchell House. These performances, a full afternoon in themselves, were followed by a complete showing of David O. Selznick's film version of *Gone with the Wind*, courtesy of Turner Entertainment Co.

The audience, of course, had all seen *Gone with the Wind* at least five times before and could hum along with the film (although they did not).

——— — ———

Garrett got a standing ovation and four verses of "Happy Birthday" by tenor Sam Hagan. Said Garrett of The Dump: "I don't know if any Atlanta architect would say that it was a great building, but the meat of the coconut is that the author of *Gone with the Wind* wrote most of her book there, and it doesn't have to be a great architectural treasure to be preserved."

After five hours of this celebration, the Garretts—Franklin and Frances—climbed into the "Red Rocket," their Oldsmobile, and hurried home to their books, trains, little dog, Dollie, and a fire in the fireplace in the kitchen, where they ate their suppers on trays.

So on to Garrett's eighty-sixth year.

Modestly, Garrett has never claimed to be a special friend of the Marshes, but in his usual words, he did know both John and Peggy (as Margaret Mitchell was known) "pleasantly."

Here are his memories of the Mitchell-Marshes:

Garrett had long been a friend and associate of the men in Margaret Mitchell's family—her father, Eugene, her uncle, Gordon, and her brother, Stephens—but he first met Margaret personally when he spent an afternoon with her in the early 1930s searching for some Indian mounds on the Cobb County side of the Chattahoochee River, across from where Peachtree Creek flows in.

Margaret had asked to join the Saturday afternoon jaunts engaged in by Beverly DuBose, Jr., Wilbur Kurtz, and Garrett, all looking for Civil War artifacts and other relics of the past.

"Inevitably," he says now, "the subject of her book came up. She said, 'You know, I'll really be happy if it sells a thousand copies.' Well, as you know, it has sold 28,000,000 copies, more than any book save the Bible. That was my first real acquaintance with Margaret Mitchell."

Earlier, however, she had telephoned Garrett from time to time while she was working on her manuscript. She wanted to be sure she wasn't using the name of any Atlanta family during the period she was writing about that had some shady history . . . "like prostitution or some other occupation that doesn't rate too high."

"Well, I could always tell her that. That was my total contribution to the writing of *Gone with the Wind*."

When the book came out, the Atlanta Historical Society, which still had rather cramped quarters, gave Margaret a reception at Rhodes Hall. Margaret's cousins Clara Mitchell McConnell and Aline Timmons, were pouring punch.

Clara Mitchell was a pretty girl, and Garrett wrangled an introduction. They started dating. Clara and her mother operated a dry goods store downtown, selling lingerie and "other accoutrements for women." Clara's mother had inherited a good deal of real estate.

"Margaret's maternal grandfather was widowed late in life, and he later married again. He then had two more children, Clara Mitchell's mother and Hughes Roberts, Sr., who was the father of Lillian Roberts. (Lillian Roberts married David Deakins, a very fine man, in the insurance business, who died a few years ago.)

"The house in which Margaret was born on Jackson Street and Cain, in an area known as Jackson Hill, was destroyed by the fire of 1917. That fire consumed everything in that block. Her grandmother Stephen's house went up in smoke too, in short order. However, they weren't living there then.

"By that time Eugene Mitchell had built the house that later became

Eugene Muse Mitchell (1866-1944) and Margaret Mitchell Marsh (1900-1946) examine a copy of Gone with the Wind *in front of the house at 1401 Peachtree Street, 1936.* Photo courtesy of the Atlanta History Center

1401 Peachtree Street. It was a very nice frame house, wide weather boarding, the third house north from the corner of Seventeenth Street as you go out Peachtree Street. I was in it many times . . . big, spacious entrance hall with big rooms opening off on each side. Margaret really grew up there from the age of twelve.

"Margaret went to public schools, then to Washington Seminary for a while, and then to Smith College. She was a student at Smith College in New England when her mother died in January 1919. So Margaret came home to run her father's house. Her father never remarried. Margaret never went back to college.

"But as she cast about for something to do, she went to work for Angus Perkerson, editor of the *Atlanta Journal* magazine section. She was employed to write feature articles, and did a good job of it.

"While she was doing that, she was thrown from a horse two or three times and had a minor automobile accident or two. (I think she was prone to accidents.) While recovering from her accidents, she could work on *GWTW*. She was living in her father's house then.

"Margaret was active socially, made her debut in 1920 or '21. She was a right-spirited young woman and did some things that the old-line dames like Mrs. Peel and Mrs. Kiser considered a little beyond the pale, like dancing one night on a table at the Driving Club, where she executed a rather risqué dance. So she never got an invitation to join the Junior League, and I think she took that very seriously.

"She did not make an appearance at the Junior League Ball, which was held the night before the movie premiere of *GWTW*, on December 14, 1939. She begged off sick. Anyway, the ball was a great success.

"I remember Cobbie Carter was president of the Junior League that year. It was black tie, quite an affair. Harry Sommers, the Chrysler dealer here, a tall, nice-looking man, led it. He came in with Margaret Palmer, Chuck Palmer's daughter. She later moved out to Nebraska. She was a pretty brunette. I took Clara Mitchell to it. . . .

"To go back a bit, Margaret was married twice. I never knew the first husband, but he was a tall, handsome man. His name was Berrien K. (Red) Upshaw. But if he had any source of income, nobody ever found out what it was. He probably bootlegged some, and he also turned out to be abusive. The marriage didn't last very long. They lived in her father's house, and both her father and her brother were sure she had made a great mistake. They didn't warm up to Upshaw at all. Her father and brother were both very conservative.

"John Marsh, who was connected with the Georgia Power Company, was in the public relations department. He was a good friend of Upshaw and turned out to be best man at Margaret's wedding to Upshaw. The marriage was the cause of considerable pain to John Marsh because he was in love with her too. Why she chose Upshaw beats me, and nearly everybody else.

"Anyway, Marsh never married anybody else, and after Margaret and Upshaw were divorced, they began to date. They were married in 1925.

"She married John Marsh at the home on Peachtree Street. It was a very nice wedding. She came down those fine steps in the entrance hall, and her second marriage was a success. John Marsh didn't enjoy very robust health. He had a bad heart and various diseases, but their marriage worked out fine. They had no children. I understand that Margaret was not particularly interested in having children.

"When they married, they moved from her father's house to what she called The Dump. It was on Tenth and Peachtree Streets. It originally faced Crescent Avenue but now faces Peachtree Street. It had been built in 1899 as a single-family home by the Sheehan family, a very good old Irish family.

"That area in the twentieth century began to develop into a neighborhood shopping center with drugstores and grocery stores, all individually owned businesses.

"She could go there to Peachtree and Tenth, go into the store of Crawford Brothers, and be waited on by a mature clerk who would walk around with her and jot down what she wanted to buy. . . . 'Ma'am, what next?' And the order would be charged and sent out.

"It was a first-class neighborhood. The Marshes lived there until they moved to the Russell Apartments.

"I didn't go to see them when they lived at The Dump. That was before I got very well acquainted with them. It was divided into six small apartments. They lived in Apartment #1, a small living room, bedroom, and kitchen, and maybe a little more space, not much. She was cramped for space when she was writing the book. Meanwhile, the book had been published.

"They moved to the Russell Apartments, which was a three-story building, beige brick, on the northeast corner of West Peachtree and Seventeenth Streets.

"They were living there when I first called on them. It was a social call. I think they lived on the second floor, stayed there until 1939, a short time before the premiere, which was December 15, 1939.

"She had sold the movie rights in 1937 for $50,000. I think she got more out of it later, but that was the original price. I've heard now that the author of *Scarlett*, Alexandra Ripley's sequel to *Gone with the Wind*, got $9,000,000 for the movie rights to *Scarlett*.

"Anyway, Margaret did sell it to the movies. She would have nothing to do with the selection of the actors and actresses, the contract stipulated that. That was a good move, because if that hadn't been in the contract, every mother in Atlanta who had a halfway good-looking daughter Scarlett's age would have been knocking on the door saying 'My daughter is the perfect person for that part,' so she saved herself a lot of trouble there, I'm sure. I have always seen the fine hand of her brother, Stephens, in that contract.

"The filming of *GWTW* was not done in Atlanta. It was all done in California. They sent two experts there so they wouldn't have a lot of anachronisms in the film. One expert was Wilbur Kurtz, who had a good knowledge of the Atlanta area, so they wouldn't show all the soil around her [Scarlett] as being dead black . . . as most of it is clay. Susan Myrick of Macon was also sent out there to be sure they used the right accents in their talk, to see they didn't talk like New Englanders in rural Georgia. That all worked out very well indeed.

"I got a letter from Margaret telling me they were going to move from the Russell Apartments to the Della Manta Apartments, which is a triangle-shaped building at the intersection of South Prado and Piedmont Avenue. It faces the intersection of the street and is sort of diagonally across from the Piedmont Driving Club tennis courts. They moved into the second floor, front, a nice building. It was built in 1920. It has been revamped with no change to its architecture . . . just cleaned up. I think there is a brass plaque on the front door saying that Margaret Mitchell once lived there. They were living there at the time of her untimely death in 1949.

Inscription by Margaret Mitchell in Franklin M. Garrett's first-edition copy of Gone with the Wind, *1936.* Photo courtesy of Franklin M. Garrett

"I didn't finish about the ball. I attended it with Clara Mitchell [McConnell]. The next night was the premiere, and I was able to get tickets to that because of my friendship with the family. It was a sell-out, of course. It was in mid-December, fairly warm for that time of year. The Grand Theater had searchlights playing on it, and the facade was rigged up to look like a handsome antebellum residence.

"Bill Hartsfield, the mayor then (and for a good many years afterward), was in his element that night, standing out in front, inviting people to come up to the mike to say a few words. The actors and actresses were all put up at the Georgian Terrace Hotel. The conspicuous absentee was Leslie Howard, who took the part of Ashley Wilkes. World War II had just started on September 1 that year. Howard was in the British Air Force and couldn't get away. I don't think he survived the war. I think he was shot down.

"The other conspicuous absentees were the black actresses and actors. In my opinion, they had done yeoman service in that film . . . Mammy and Prissy and Big John . . . remember, that was in 1939. The Georgian Terrace did not entertain any black guests then.

"As everybody knows, *Gone with the Wind* plays heavily on the emotions. I will never forget the silence that followed the end of the movie that night. You could have heard a pin drop on the carpet. . . . No stomping of feet, whistling, or loud noises. . . . Everybody got up and walked quietly out.

"That was followed by what was characterized as a typical plantation breakfast . . . the elegant type. It was held in the handsome ballroom of the Piedmont Driving Club. I took Clara Mitchell to that too. I think we got home about 3:30 in the morning.

"After Margaret Mitchell became so well known . . . one of the best presidents we ever had at the Driving Club was DeSales Harrison. He served in 1939 and 1940. He didn't know John Marsh well, but he knew that I knew them. He said to me, 'You know, the Marshes ought to be members here.' They had to be invited. He told me to sound them out to see if they wanted to join. They were very receptive. They really weren't very interested in big social affairs, but they lived right across the street, and they liked to walk over and have lunch at the Driving Club. So they joined, and John Marsh was a member until his death in 1952.

"They knew by that time that the book was a success. They didn't live conspicuously and never moved out of that apartment. They were living there on the hot August night in 1949, and John was not well. Margaret had to kind of nurse him along, but he felt well enough to go out this night and see a movie. They headed for the Arts Theater on the northeast corner of Thirteenth and Peachtree Streets. The attraction that night was *The Canterbury Tales.*

"Neither of them got a chance to see it. They drove over through Ansley Park, I guess it was about three-quarters of a mile, and parked right across the street from the theater, in a small parking lot that had been the site of the Robert L. Foreman home.

"That reminds me that Robert Foreman was Trott Foreman's father. Trott had lived for many years on West Paces Ferry Road next door to the cemetery on Chatham Road. One day I asked him if he had any objection to living next door to a cemetery. He said, 'No, I don't. I don't get any empty paper cups, beer cans, or noise.' I think Fluffy McDuffie lives there now . . . a nice alliterative name, isn't it?

"Back to the Marshes. The Marshes started to walk across Peachtree Street. There was a great difference in their height. About halfway across the street, Margaret noticed a car approaching at a high rate of speed. She broke away from John, left him standing there in the middle of the street, and undertook to run back to their car. That was fatal. The off-duty taxi driver who was at the wheel of the approaching car . . . his name was Hugh Dorsey Gravitt . . . claimed that he was hurrying to get a prescription for a sick baby. Be that as it may, it resulted in a collision, fatally for Margaret. She was taken to Grady Hospital, where she got the best of attention, but passed away five days later on August 16, 1949 . . . Gravitt was arrested, charged with involuntary manslaughter, and served a while in jail.

"So ended the life of the author of *GWTW*. The funeral was held at Spring Hill, which had been built by Mr. Patterson in 1928. You had to have an engraved invitation to get in to the service. I think the reason for that was that many well-meaning people who were curiosity seekers would have crowded the place.

"I remember the funeral service very well. I got an engraved invitation and still have it. The funeral service was preached by Dean Raimundo de Ovies of the Cathedral of St. Philip, and then the funeral procession wound through the older streets of Atlanta to Oakland Cemetery.

"There are several Mitchell lots at Oakland. Steve has one, his father has one. Margaret and John are buried on a lot with Mr. and Mrs. Mitchell, Margaret's mother and father. There is a little baby's grave in the corner of that lot. So there are five graves there. There is a marker on the grave, Mitchell on one side, Marsh on the other.

"John survived Margaret only three years. He died in 1952.

"The lot is very well kept. It is quite a tourist attraction. I think more visitors want to see that grave than any others, including Bobby Jones, several former mayors, several governors, and three or four generals in the Civil War.

"People ask me what I think about the sequel to *GWTW*, and I tell them I certainly had no objection to one being written, because *Gone with the Wind* sort of leaves you up in the air. You remember the ending: 'My dear, I don't give a damn,' and people have always wondered whether they would ever have gotten back together.

"I never heard Margaret say whether she was going to write a sequel or was not going to.

"I have read the sequel, have a first edition of it, autographed. I didn't enjoy it as much as *Gone with the Wind*, as much of the action of *Scarlett* is in Ireland and a good bit in Charleston. And, of course, my orientation is Atlanta. I can soak up Atlanta locations like a sponge, because I can get a mental picture of any localities that might be mentioned. And even the new book *Scarlett* leaves us a bit in a fog. You don't know whether they ever got reconciled and married. A lot of people in Atlanta refused even to read *Scarlett,* but I bet they did.

"I don't think Margaret would have objected to the treatment."

―――― ― ――――

In the epilogue of *Atlanta and Environs,* Garrett summed up the death of Margaret Mitchell with this touching and sensitive paragraph:

"On the morning of August 18, 1949, at beautiful Spring Hill, Dean Raimundo de Ovies, in the black and white vestments of his office, read the service for the dead from the *Book of Common Prayer.* Then, as the cortege moved slowly through the streets to the ancient and hollowed precincts of Oakland Cemetery, the sorrow and grief of a native populace became starkly evident . . . in the blank, stricken countenances of every-day Atlantans, white and colored, who lined the curb and stood on porches and in windows and doorways, to gaze silently upon the last journey of a great lady. . . ."

1993

Garrett Honored with His Own Everlasting Shining Light

On October 15, 1993, Franklin Miller Garrett became the twenty-sixth Atlantan to receive the prestigious Shining Light Award, given jointly by the Atlanta Gas Light Company and WSB-Radio.

A tall black lamppost with an everlasting flame encased within its octagonal globe was lighted at the entrance of the Walter McElreath Hall. McElreath Hall houses the archives and library and administrative offices, as well as the Robert Woodruff Auditorium and other public areas of the Historical Society.

A plaque on the Shining Light reads "In honor of Franklin M. Garrett, Official Historian, the Atlanta Historical Society, City of Atlanta and Fulton County, Author of *Atlanta and Environs*," adding the dedicatory words "In honoring the past, he inspired the present, To serve the Future." It is signed by two corporate donors who instituted this award in 1969.

Another plaque, this one a few feet away, on the facade of McElreath Hall also recognizes Garrett as one of the persons responsible for the construction of the building itself in 1975. That plaque also honors Beverly M.

DuBose, Jr., as president of the Atlanta Historical Society at that time, and the building committee: William A. Parker (chairman), Mrs. Ivan Allen, Jr., Franklin Garrett, and Virlyn Moore, Jr.

In nominating Garrett for this award, Kenneth I. Parker of Acworth wrote: "Mr. Garrett has served Atlanta and Georgia as custodian of our past. The historical chronicles he has written will live long after him. His words are more than a mere record of what has gone before, but an understanding of the past as a vision into the future. The Atlanta Historical Society, guided by Mr. Garrett, is a living laboratory for all of us to experience the way our parents and grandparents lived, worked and played."

The presentation speeches themselves were especially admiring. Speaking for WSB-Radio, with which he was associated as general manager and public voice for years, Elmo I. Ellis said: "Because he is such a towering person in our midst, nearly everybody in Atlanta knows Franklin Garrett. More astounding, however, is the fact that Franklin Garrett knows nearly everybody in Atlanta . . . just as he also knows every street, avenue, and alleyway . . . every school, hospital, church, synagogue, and cemetery.

"Franklin's tireless, research efforts . . . his voluminous writing and the speeches he delivers a hundred or more times a year, have made him a unique and irreplaceable resource. Yet he gladly shared his knowledge with unfailing generosity.

"Since he has enlightened and inspired us for so many years, our friend Franklin deserves all the thanks and applause we can give . . . it is proper that we salute him today."

His erstwhile colleague at Coca-Cola, Donald R. Greene, president of The Coca-Cola Foundation, added his tribute:

"I'm pleased to say that I can claim at least three common bonds with Franklin Garrett. We both serve on the board of Atlanta Landmarks, which owns and operates the Fox Theatre. Second, we both have worked at Coca-Cola in the public information/public relations office. But most importantly we both met our wives at the office when they too were employees of The Coca-Cola Company.

"So, Frances and Franklin, I'm particularly pleased to be here today to tell you and this gathering how thrilled the Coca-Cola family is to be able to celebrate your receiving the Shining Light Award. And on behalf of Roberto Goizueta, he asked me to convey to you that this award is richly deserved.

"A goodly number of us at Coca-Cola today began our careers in the shadow of Franklin Garrett. He became a legend in his own time in the halls of The Coca-Cola Company. Early on, his love of history was put to good use. Franklin researched and wrote one of the earliest chronicles of the company, produced in the years before World War II. And Franklin was responsible for helping shape the company's role in community affairs.

"By shining his light, by caring for our past, Franklin inspires the present to serve the future."

For his part Garrett was for once particularly speechless. He said: "I know all the men and women who have this award from the first one. I am more than honored to be among their company."

The "honored company" of award winners was indeed outstanding: Dr. George M. Sparks, H. O. Smith, Margaret Mitchell, Mary Givens Bryan, Dr. J. Elliott Scarborough, Dr. Rufus O. Clement, Ivan Allen, Sr., J. Arch Avary, William B. Hartsfield, Ralph McGill, Dr. Philip Weltner, Robert W. Woodruff, John A. Sibley, Henry L. Bowden, D. W. Brooks, Robert Tyre "Bobby" Jones, Jr., Mrs. Mae Maxwell Yates, Ben W. Fortson, Jr., Dr. Benjamin E. Mays, Dean Rusk, Pollard Turman, Mrs. Leonard "Be" Haas, Dr. Leila Daughtry-Denmark, A. B. Padgett, S. Truett Cathy, and Charles Longstreet Weltner.

CHAPTER 23

An Office That Evolved—Almost a Museum

With no business machines whatever, except, of course a telephone, Franklin Garrett runs a full-service information bureau from his office in the McElreath Hall Building.

"I get calls every day from the press, radio, or TV people who are doing an article on such and such a subject. They call me as a shortcut. Of course, if I can answer their question, that saves them a lot of research. Hardly a day goes by that some of these calls are not from newspaper people, business magazines, or general magazines. . . .

"Another one of my functions is answering questions by mail from people who want to know about some ancestor . . . so, of course, I answer a great many letters from the public. If they come personally to the Society wanting something about family history, they are sent to me. Sometimes this involves just answering when this or that was built or that sort of thing. I do handle a rather heavy correspondence. I like to get inquiries because sometimes I get information I have been looking for a long time.

"If I can't get back to them right away, I ask Lil Salter to do it for them. She can answer most questions too. Her daughter, Anne, is in charge of our library/archives department and very capable.

Garrett's office, tucked into a snug corner of the lower floor of the McElreath Hall looks out on a little glade of green with shafts of sun-

Franklin M. Garrett presiding in his office at the Atlanta History Center, 1988.
William F. Hull, photographer. Photo courtesy of the Atlanta History Center

light sharpening the view. He stands at the window often, enjoying it
and thinking.

In 1996, when most offices are characterized by significant humming
as occupants stare intently at computer screens, their hands resting on
keyboards, Garrett's office is busy and even noisy at moments. Clocks
strike, bells tinkle, and little whistles emit shrill sounds, most of this on
his command. This is an office that evolved. Garrett's life's work has added
trophies and tokens; they have all been carefully installed in his business
venue. It is full of mementoes: small sculptured busts, portraits, awards,
gifts, sentimental plaques. It is really a three-dimensional album or scrapbook, almost a private museum in itself. Every item seems to recall a pleasant day in his life.

He walks around the small space with a visitor.

"Now about this clock. It's an English cathedral clock given to the Historical Society as a gift by Mr. and Mrs. Samuel Greenblatt. . . . The reason it is here, it didn't fit the right period for the Swan House, so I gave
it a home. And incidentally, it needs winding. . . .

"It is carved walnut, with a London imprint, some other engraving on
it. It strikes quarter hour, half hour, three-quarters hour, and then the hour.
Let me wind it.

"Oh, the bell, the locomotive bell? (He strikes it, and it clangs loud-
ly.) That bell is off of a steam locomotive belonging to the Russians in
World War I. You remember the Russians finally collapsed during the war.
This bell was in Southampton at that time, so the Russians couldn't take
it back home. The Missouri Pacific Railroad bought it, and it was used
on one of their locomotives until the diesel came in. It was given to the
Historical Society by a gentleman whose name I don't recall at this
moment, so I gave it a home. It is solid brass. It stays polished, I'm glad
to say.

"That's Mr. Eugene M. Mitchell. He was Margaret Mitchell's father,
and as you see he lived from 1866 to 1944. He was born here in Atlanta,
a lawyer by profession. I served as one of his pallbearers in 1944. So many
of my old friends are gone.

"This portrait was by Glascock Reynolds. I think Glascock's wife was
a relative of the Mitchells.

"Here, the Civil War Round Table, of which I was a founding member, designated me as an honorary member in recognition of forty years of 'outstanding service.' . . . That sounds pretty good. It was given to me when Claude Hamrick of Marietta was president of the Round Table.

"Now this is the Maynard Jackson Proclamation. I'm not sure whose idea it was, but I was very flattered that it happened . . . that a day would be named for me. The date was February 14, 1970. *Franklin M. Garrett Day.*

——— — ———

Garrett's Lowdown on Atlanta Mayors

On October 30, 1989, Garrett informed the Rotary Club of Atlanta that Ivan Allen, Jr., was one of Atlanta's most able mayors, and that. . . . Jonathan Norcross from Maine, one of several Atlanta mayors from the North, represented the Law and Order Party, beating a candidate from the Rowdy Party. . . . William Ezzard, who lived to the age of eighty-seven, was the only Atlanta mayor to serve both before and after the Civil War. . . . James M. Calhoun served during the Civil War and had the distinction of being the only mayor to surrender Atlanta to an invading army.

Captain James W. English was a mayor, Confederate veteran, businessman, and banker who always asked whether customers were "puttin' in or takin' out" when they came into his bank. . . . James G. Woodward, running one time for re-election, was a successful primary candidate. But after being arrested, when running in a general election for being intoxicated, exclaimed that "my doctor prescribed the alcohol." He was defeated. . . . Robert F. Maddox advanced $75,000 in personal funds to buy a new city hall, and Asa G. Candler paid personally for a city water line to a World War I army camp. . . . William Hartsfield served as Atlanta's mayor for twenty-one years, longer than any other person.

——— — ———

"Now this is from the President's Council of Atlanta; 'Official Historian of the City of Atlanta and Fulton County, Georgia, with the sincere appreciation for time taken to share Atlanta history and for unselfish dedication and outstanding service to the city of Atlanta. Signed: President of the Council, with love and respect, Dr. Millard L. Kimbrough, Secretary, March 19, 1992.'

"Now this rolltop desk was purchased by The Coca-Cola Company for the use of its then general counsel, Robert Troutman, of the well-known King and Spalding firm. Originally I think he was with Troutman and Troutman. He decided to leave his office at The Coca-Cola Company and go downtown, and for some reason I needed a desk. This one had been put in storage. I, of course, liked the desk. I used it for several years, and then when I took early retirement from Coke and came out here, I thought it would be nice if the desk could follow me along. So I asked that it be given to the Atlanta Historical Society. I believe Paul Austin was president then and okayed that. It was given to the AHS, and I will use it as long as I am here.

"Those books on top of it . . . I'm included in *Who's Who in the Southeast*, and this is the two-volume set of *Atlanta and Environs* that I did write. Original print, of course, and here is the volume which I did not write . . . the volume on personalities and leaders. The University [of Georgia] Press has reprinted this two or three times since it first came out in 1954. Next year it will have been in print forty years.

"This painting and the other one hanging beneath it were done for the Trust Company of Georgia a long time ago . . . by an Atlanta artist, Lewis Gregg. I don't know how many were in the set, must have been twenty-five or thirty of them. They adorned the lobby of the Old Trust Company of Georgia building. Then they built a new building, much more *moderne,* and gave most of the set to us.

"This one of Henry Grady is in the Grady room at the Commerce Club. And this one is of William McIntosh, who signed the treaty of Indian Springs giving the state of Georgia a vast tract of land. It was in 1821 . . . that included the site of Atlanta. His mother was Cherokee and his father was a Scotsman. Then he continued giving away land, and after he had given away a lot of it, in 1826 in Carroll County . . . his people got mad because he had given away so much land (he had a house in Carroll County . . . it is marked, but it is right on the line), a group of Indians surrounded his home, set the house on fire, and when he ran out of the house, they shot him dead. As you see, he lived for fifty years. A fine-looking mantle he has on . . . an interesting head-piece with a plume and almost a crown . . . very colorful.

"I have two of these the Trust Company gave the AHS. . . . The other one is George M. Troup, for whom Troup County was named . . . and of course LaGrange is the county seat.

"This is a little plaque . . . this was in 1986 . . . for making a speech. A reproduction of Lincoln in the Washington-Lincoln memorial . . . Manufacturers Sales Executive Club plaque . . . that was in 1974, and the American Institute of Plant Engineers . . . that was given to me in 1983 for making a speech. Former Pennsylvania Railroad Calendar [large framed picture]. Presumably on the Washington-New York line.

"Here is the Rotary Club award. . . . One is given every year to the member who performs the most outstanding public service during the last year. It was an honor.

"This is the map of the city of Atlanta in 1871 . . . very graphically shows the various areas of Atlanta, including the center of the city.

"That's a Newcomen Society of North America award they gave me. . . . Their business is the study of natural history. This certifies that I have been elected to membership. They have a meeting in Atlanta from time to time.

"That's my Rotary membership. Here is an award of merit for collecting, researching, presenting, and promoting the history of Atlanta . . . from American State and Local History of 1981 . . .

"Here's a framed resolution 'universally recognized as the outstanding historian for the city of Atlanta . . . author of *Atlanta and Environs*, throughout career, unselfishly have shared time and knowledge with students and public in general, and have served as constant source of inspiration for the preserving of historical knowledge . . . outstanding citizen of Atlanta . . . worked long and faithfully on behalf of numerous civic organizations . . . throughout the metropolitan area.' That was signed by Sam Massell, mayor, 1973, December 17, 1973.

"That's a reproduction of the Atlanta telephone directory for 1881 . . . required only one page.

"That's a top picture from the New York Central Railroad calendar, May 19, 1938. It's a picture of the Twentieth Century Limited, eastbound and westbound train passing each other just outside Buffalo, New York. I have a nice model of one of these in my library.

"Below it, the Pennsylvania Railroad calendar, must have been about 1940, with a train being pulled by a steam locomotive and the other a diesel. These are big calendars . . . thirty-six or forty inches. . . .

"Now this principal's desk . . . it belongs to the Historical Society. I bought that when I came out here as director. Also this chair. . . . That belongs to the Historical Society. I've been in it quite a while.

"Three top pictures are reproductions of Currier and Ives prints. They did many prints on railroad subjects, most in the 1860s, '70s, along in there.

"Here is an ODK . . . May 4, 1969 . . . 'in recognition of his conspicuous attainments in service in collegiate activities, the Omicron Delta Kappa this day . . . Georgia State College.'

"'The Atlanta Chapter of the American Institute of Architects . . . through both writing and personal efforts . . . and for dedication to the preservation of that history.'

"Now these debs you're standing here with . . . I was the Grand Marshal . . . that sounds big . . . Cotillion Club, 1985.

"That's Lafayette, the Frenchman who came over here in the Revolution to help us out. . . . That is a copy of the original painting by Samuel F. B. Morse, also the inventor of the telegraph. The original is in the City Hall of the city of New York. It's on loan to me by Mr. and Mrs. Joe M. Almand. He has passed away. If they want it back, I will give it to them.

"That large silver tureen belongs to the Historical Society. . . . 'Miss Jessie Muse, a scholar with broad knowledge . . . respected by her pupils is admired and loved by associates . . . of Girls High School.' Some of the girls referred to her as Miss Messie Juse.

"This little porcelain . . . it seems to me Frank Maier gave us a set of those.

"This is a major of the Regiment T. in 1776 . . . Revolutionary military. This is Judge Julius Hillyer. . . . He was the father of the late Henry and Georgia Hillyer in Atlanta. It is a steel engraving. They show every detail. I just hung it there because I liked the picture.

"Here is an award from the Woodrow Wilson College of Law. . . . 'Presents the Governor Walker citation for distinguished service to Franklin Miller Garrett, distinguished graduate of the Woodrow Wilson College of Law, Class of 1941. . . . Presented June 12, 1976 . . . Foremost historian, author of *Atlanta and Environs* . . . author of *Yesterday's Atlanta,* author of many articles on Atlanta, and editor of the Historical Bulletin of the Atlanta Historical Society, President of the Atlanta Historical Society, official historian of the city of Atlanta, and Coca-Cola Company.' Given to me by Virlyn Moore.

"That's my diploma from Woodrow Wilson School of Law, dated in 1941, signed by Clifford Walker and Joe Kilbride.

"This is a map of Atlanta in 1938 . . . showing location of Civil War troops on a modern map. . . . That was done by the Atlanta Chamber of Commerce, and I acquired one from them. Historical data was provided by the late Wilbur Kurtz.

"Here is another award . . . grand marshal of the Centennial Christmas Parade.

Awards

In May 1970, Garrett was awarded a doctorate of humane letters from Oglethorpe College.

In 1973, by resolution of the Board of Aldermen of Atlanta, Garrett was named official historian of Atlanta.

In 1975, he was named official historian of Fulton County by the Fulton County Commission.

In 1985, he was given the Meritorious Public Service Medal by the National Association of Secretaries of State.

In 1989, he was named Paul Harris Fellow by the Rotary Foundation of Rotary International.

In 1993, Rotary Atlanta gave him the Armin Maier award for "unselfish service to his city over the years." Commented John E. Smith II, in making the award, "I don't believe I can add anything that hasn't already been said. . . . Another star in your crown. We don't have time for you to recite the Wabash Cannonball. . . ."

—— — ——

"That's a little cartoon, a take-off on Jimmy Carter. By a Miss Pilgreen of Pilgreen's Restaurant.

"Up there is a beautiful picture of the state capitol of Georgia . . . with the General Gordon equestrian statute there in the foreground. I think that was gotten out on the one hundredth anniversary of the building, which would have been in 1989.

"A portrait of Garrett . . . done by a woman who lives in St. Augustine, Florida, whom I have never met. She asked for some information. I handled the matter. I didn't ask her to do this . . . and one day the painting just appeared here. So there it is. She's deceased now. She did a very nice portrait of Scarlett O'Hara . . . at least how she thought she would look. . . . We have that one at home.

"That's a photograph of me standing at one of the entrances to the Swan House holding one of the volumes of *Atlanta and Environs*. That picture was taken by Kenneth Rogers . . . the *Constitution*'s great photographer.

"This is Miss Ruth Blair and Mayor Hartsfield when she was Woman of the Year in 1956. She's a fine-looking woman. I always liked the mayor, too. Her dates were 1889 and 1974. He was born in 1890 and died in 1971.

"Here are Mr. and Mrs. Garrett. They're all dressed up . . . he in cummerbund . . . she is in a chiffon dress. It says 'Happy Birthday' from Susan Hodges. She ran the Swan House for several years.

"Here it seems are four awards . . . Delta Air Lines making me a Flying Colonel. 'I don't do much for them, except brag about them in speeches.' The Cobb County Board of Realtors, 1977. A special award in 1975 from the Dixie Council of Authors and Journalists . . . 'whose lifelong dedication to recording Atlanta's history has furnished a rich store of knowledge for future generations. . . .'

"Here is a little picture of a Civil War locomotive . . . a colorful little print . . . looks like a toy.

"That is a Wilbur Kurtz painting of Colonel R. J. Lowry arriving at the Driving Club about 1900, in his tallyho. There is a larger painting of the same subject over the main bar at the Driving Club. . . . Kurtz painting is owned by the Historical Society, but I like it, so it is in my office. That is a four-horse coach . . . a tallyho. . . .

"This is a lithograph showing a view of the Atlanta public square at the time of the Civil War. . . . Central Presbyterian Church and Second Baptist church are shown.

"That's an award from the American Legion, Fulton Post 134, in 1980, naming Garrett 'Legionnaire of the Year.'

"This is a Georgia Genealogical Society appreciation award.

"And this is an award from the Mental Health Association of Metropolitan Atlanta, date 1987.

"This is a photo of Walter McElreath, and this is a bronze bust of Henry Grady.

"That is a doorknob from the Trust Company of Georgia Building, formerly the Equitable Building.

"This is a certificate of appreciation from CCFA . . . I don't know the whole title . . . and this is an award from the National League of American Pen Women, Inc., to Dr. F. M. Garrett, to encourage 'achievement in letters, music composition, and to the fine arts, to encourage the creative arts in Georgia.'

"Here is an award from the city of College Park, honoring F. M. Garrett Day in that community as grand marshal of the Centennial Parade of College Park in 1991.

"Fulton County passed a resolution naming Garrett historian of Fulton County.

"This is a *Saturday Evening Post* cover I liked . . . it is a Norman Rockwell. And this is a painting by Gilbert Grant of a Confederate soldier on picket duty.

"This, as you can see, is a banjo clock. I just like it.

"This is a *Who's Who* publication . . . Marquis . . . and this is the Rotary Club's outstanding citizen award in 1983.

"No reason for this small bust of Shakespeare 'Immortal Bard.' . . . Just liked it."

Garrett then tells the story about George M. Ingersoll, the famous agnostic, who commented when he heard that John Calvin had died the

Mamie Eisenhower, unidentified, Franklin M. Garrett, and Lil Salter following a visit by Mrs. Eisenhower to the Swan House, 1971. Photo courtesy of the Atlanta History Center

day Shakespeare was born: "What a glorious exchange!"

Two sentimental additions: needlepoint pillows from Frances, his wife, who is a fine handicraft artist, and a very special lamp given to Garrett by his son and daughter for Christmas.

The lamp is an old-time locomotive, which performs nobly—switches on, whistle blows, headlights come on, smoke comes out of the stack, puffs like a steam engine. "I like this especially," he says warmly. "I show it to all my visitors."

Just outside this little hall-of-fame office sits Garrett's secretary, Lil Salter, a friend of more than fifty years, at her trusty old typewriter. She is smart, staunch, and as fragile as a leaf.

Lil Salter suspects that Franklin Garrett is the ultimate gentleman in the world.

CHAPTER 24

The Happiest Room in Garrett's House — His Library

The serious little boy who wanted books more than toys, who was more interested in people than in games, and who followed every street and road from its beginning to its end looking for wonders it might reveal has concentrated all his imagination on his impressive home library. It is considered by many to be the finest private historical library in the area.

Chosen thoughtfully and often sacrificially, the Garrett library has evolved over his whole lifetime. Many of the books have long been out of print and are valued as very rare books by professional collectors. The library encompasses thousands of volumes, grouped in subjects or types of work, thirteen complete encyclopedias, biographies of all the presidents, histories of many cities, and an entire room of Atlanta and Georgia records.

In his library, Franklin Garrett is at home with all these books, as much at ease as if they were his lifetime friends. (He does not countenance the suggestion that today's compact discs hold as many as thirty-five hundred books on each disc, or that the *Encyclopedia Britannica* is recorded on one single disc with room to spare. He is a little hard of hearing and such vulgar and common reporting is ignored as irrelevant.)

Franklin M. Garrett in the library at his home, Mainline Three, ca. 1990. Bush Enos, photographer. Photo courtesy of Franklin M. Garrett

He holds with Thomas Carlyle, who said long ago that the true university of these days is a collection of books. Garrett has built his life on that and the association of learned and inspired men and women.

Whatever his philosophy, Garrett is happier in his library than in any room of his home. He says so. He knows every volume, exactly where it is supposed to be in the room, its rank on the shelves, and what it contains between its covers.

We walk around the room, which is really divided into two room, and is an entire wing of his house.

"Both rooms combined would be about forty-five feet this way (long) and about twenty feet wide. The ceilings are ten feet. They have six shelves, two shelves deep, plus cabinets at the bottom. My architect was one of the best. He was Clement J. Ford, and my builder was Robert Goodsell. When Goodsell builds a house, he builds it to last a while. Ford and I are the same age. He was born on September 13 and

I on the twenty-fifth of the same month. I said 'Sir' to him because he was older. I respect age.

"Anyway, I had to build a new house, because my house on Roxboro Road, which I had built to live in the rest of my life (where I could watch the trains go by), was gone. MARTA took it. So I knew I would have to build one because I wouldn't have found a house already built that would take my library.

"This space is divided into two rooms. Let's go this way around it. I don't like paperbacks at all. They won't open wide enough. I'm interested in the history of cities. . . . Here is the *History of the City of New York* and *Baltimore: City and County*, and up there is a copy of *Tobacco Road* and Richard Wright's *Native Son*.

"Of course I'm interested in Atlanta primarily, but the growth of cities fascinates me. Up there on the top are the Van Wyck works, which are charming to read.

"Here's a set on the history of the South gotten out by one of the university presses—*Southern Colonies in the 17th Century* is the first one. The peculiar thing about this set is . . . yes, the University of Louisiana Press. Merton Coulter wrote this one. He didn't write all of these. As I said, the peculiar thing about this set is the man who was supposed to write volume 2, never wrote, it, so there is no volume 2. It's a sort of duke's mixture. Herbert Asbury's books . . . I find those most interesting. He writes about the lower life in big cities . . . the Bowery and that sort of thing. So, well, it is a sort of miscellany.

"Here, one panel down, there is *New York, Detroit, Chicago, South Street*, which is a maritime history of New York, *Philadelphia, Watson's Annals* in three volumes, *Great Bridges* (the Brooklyn Bridge), *Beacon Hill*, that would be about Boston, *History of the National Capitol*, W. B. Bryan, and *Cleveland*. That is just reading right along on one panel.

"Down here is *St. Louis, Philadelphia,* and *Louisville.* Underneath here is a full cabinet of books. Currier and Ives printed all their catalogues in 1936. I have every one of them. The rural scenes are very restful. Makes me feel good looking at them. And here is the New York City directory for 1833. I have every one of those. They're interesting to refer to. I like to read the magazine *Antiques*. They are always referring to silversmiths and other skilled artisans in New York. I like to look them up and see how they have been listed.

"I have the first directory of Washington, D.C., 1822, when James Monroe was president. He is listed like everyone else: James Monroe, at the President's House.

"In this corner are books about Atlanta and the South. I couldn't quite get them all in here. Here are two or three histories of the Cotton States and International Exposition of 1895 and other books pertaining to our area.

"Here is Henry Grady's *New South*. Here is the *Architecture* of Neel Reid and Lewis Edmund Crook, Jr., who was living up to a short time ago. Here is *The Art of the Old South*, and here is Elizabeth Dowling's book *American Classics*. I think that's a biography of Philip Shutze. Profusely illustrated.

"Here is *Richmond Today*. You see, Richmond is my father's home, so I've got a lot of valuable books here. One of my friends at The Coca-Cola Company noticed a history of Baltimore. He said, 'Whatya got that for?' Well, I didn't try to explain it. (Mr. Garrett's mother was reared in Baltimore.)

"Dictionaries . . . I refer to dictionaries frequently. Here is one *Dictionary of American Biography*. It is a standard work. There are more volumes now than when I bought this set. This is an encyclopedia put out by Colliers. I like the binding. I use that frequently. I wanted a little information about Mary, Queen of Scots, who, if you will pardon my language, was a real bitch. She was finally executed.

"And B. J. Lossing, his books on the wars are classics. Here is his *History of the Revolution, the War of 1812*, first editions of both of them, and up here is the *History of Society*. There is one by Ward McAllister of New York City. Over there is *The Perennial Philadelphians* and *Fifth Avenue*, and over there are books by Fisk, who was an eminent American historian . . . *Old Virginia and Her Neighbors*, *The American Revolution*, and *The Beginning of New England*, so those are good items.

"We need ladders to climb up to the top shelves. Here is *The History of the United States*, eight volumes in that . . . by Rhodes, I think. It's sort of a landmark in American history.

"Most books today have dust jackets. If the dust jacket is attractive to me, I'll leave it on. But I save the dust jackets, because if this library is ever sold, it will increase the value of it. Now there have been several books written about the lost historical markers in cities and those are fascinating. Here is *Lost London, Lost America, Lost Boston*, picturing old buildings and landmarks that no longer exist.

"I guess I do have a big investment here. But I don't regret it at all. *The Appleton Encyclopedia of American Biography* was a standard work for many years, and it is still good. These books are bound in leather-calf, beautifully done. Many of the full-page illustrations are steel engravings. Now Thomas Hart Benton . . . he was a hard fellow to deal with. He was a statesman of Missouri.

"I'm very fond of architecture. Here is a history of the firm of McKim, Mead, and White. They were the architects of New York's Grand Central Station . . . among other famous buildings.

"This beautifully bound book called *Picturesque America* is quite a book. I bought that in New York, and in the process of moving, the binding got rubbed a little.

"I read sitting down, propped up if I am reading in bed. Here is a set on American rivers, published by Putnam . . . *The Hudson, The St. Lawrence, The Mississippi, The Niagara, The Connecticut,* and here I have a complete set of *Who Was Who in America.* I frequently refer to those, with an index to all volumes. They cover all the people who have been in *Who's Who in America* and are now deceased.

This man, Mark Sullivan, was a notable historian. I have his complete set of books called *Our Times,* six of those. They were published from the turn of the century to the '20s or so.

"There's a good many histories of companies here . . . published by the House of Harper and the *Atlantic Monthly* . . . Neiman Marcus, Hartford Insurance Company, Macy's, The East India Company, etc.

"Now, practically everything in this area is about railroads, and a few books on ships. . . . There is one on the history of airplanes, though I am not terrific on airplanes. . . . I realize their great value to the economy and all that, but I can't get excited about them. I think one reason is that I deplore destruction . . . and airplanes have been responsible for much of it in dropping bombs. That rubs me the wrong way. I have many individual histories of many railroads here, and you will notice that I have many models on model tracks . . . Pennsylvania, New York Central, they all work.

"Here are some little badges Frances's brother-in-law gave me. They are badges of railroad security police. That's a railroad watch, and this is a porter's badge . . . and a Western and Atlantic railroad switch key. There used to be a lot of private owners' refrigerators on railroads, holding perishable goods. The Cudahy Packing Company had one. They made Old Dutch Cleanser, and in 1933 some politician passed a law prohibiting the use of advertising on cars used in interchange of one or more railroads, and the reason was the smaller shippers couldn't afford this. . . ."

"Those green and red volumes are official guides to the railroads. They are the ticket agent's bible. They began publication in 1868, and they include all the other railroads' maps, lists of officers of the railroads, etc. You see, I have a mania for getting everything complete. So I want one for each year, and that is what I have. . . . They go back to 1868.

"I had a call not long ago from a gentleman who wanted to know what time a certain train went through Dacula, Georgia, which is between Lawrenceville and Athens. So all I had to do . . . the year was 1904. So I got the book for 1904, which I have, and looked it up and could give him the information right off the bat. I've got all the Seaboard time tables. . . . I will show you those. . . .

"This old desk is a beautiful thing. It was in the state capitol in Milledgeville and is said to have been used by Gov. Joe Brown. I can't prove that. It was certainly of that period. I keep it open like this. . . . This goes in and this comes down . . . like that.

"Now this painting . . . got it in Marshall Fields in Chicago when I was furnishing the house on Roxboro Road. The painter was A. L. Grace. I have told you before that I am sort of old-fashioned. I like music with a lilt . . . art that is intelligible, and poetry that rhymes.

"I think those two pictures are interesting. The top one is a little boy with his toy train, a locomotive . . . with this great big piece of machinery, wondering what makes it go. I have a feeling this little fellow grew up to be interested in trains. The picture below was a typical locomotive engineering passenger service in the years before World War II.

"The reason these Currier and Ives prints are here . . . I look at them once a year. Langdon Quin always furnishes me with his company's calendar. There are twelve of them each year, and they go back to 1936.

"All of the things on this desk have some significance . . . at least to me. They were given to me after some speech, usually. I make about a hundred speeches a year. I have a list of all the organizations I have spoken to.

"Over here is all biography. I have biographies of all the presidents of the United States . . . I think up to Carter. These busts, they are the busts of the presidents (I have them in front of the books about the men), they are arranged alphabetically rather than in their term of office. Here's James Madison. They are bronze, very heavy, and at the base is the name of the president they depict and the dates he served as president. I think they are very attractive. I collected these one at a time. You know quite often things are sold like that now . . . plates, etc. . . . you start in, and they send you one a month.

"The rest of the shelves hold biographies, everything from Nero to Casey Jones. Jeb Stuart, John Trumbull, Joseph Smith, Abraham Lincoln, William E. Barton, Ida Tarbell, Carl Sandburg's set on Lincoln, Mary, wife of Lincoln, published in 1928.

"Now I do have a biography of Carter called *Keeping Faith* and the little bronze figure of him in front of his book.

"Here is Adlai Stevenson . . . Lydia Pinkham, Billy the Kid, and Charles Wilson Peale . . . four volumes of John Marshall, one of the best lawyers we ever had, chief justice of the Supreme Court.

"These plates are paintings of famous homes. . . . This one is Jefferson Davis's home Beauvoir on the gulf coast between Biloxi and some other city. This one over here is Henry Clay's home in Kentucky, Ashland, and this set consisted of fourteen plates, some of them in the living room.

"Here is a complete set of Washington Irving's works. This is a Wilbur Kurtz painting. A lot of the literature is in the living room in that big breakfront and on those shelves. Here is a set of French porcelains. I just liked the color. It says: 'Gallio Louis France.'

"Over here it is all biography: a first edition of Freeman's four-volume set of *Robert E. Lee*. Over here is Wild Bill Hickok . . . Ernest Hemingway, Gen. Nathan Forrest, Jay Cook, Benjamin Franklin, Timothy Flint. . . . I've collected faster than I could read.

"People come in here and say, 'Have you read 'em all?' You know, you don't read them all at one time . . . you use them for reference. I don't waste them by rushing through them till I am looking for something and find it. Here is a book on Alec Stephens of Crawfordville, Georgia, and *The Life and Times of Cotton Mather.*

"I get a special edition book catalogue from time to time. I check just the ones I have glanced through, and the total came to $3,400 and something.

"I bind magazines that I value . . . for instance, I have *Time* magazine bound all the way back to January 1936. I have a complete set of *Life* magazines, complete set of the magazine *Antiques*. They keep on coming out. . . . I'll probably run out of space, if not out of time. Here is an interesting cover of *Time* with the big four of that time . . . here it is, August 15, 1955. The Big Four were Anthony Eden, General Eisenhower, Joseph McCarthy, and the fourth one is Stalin . . . see the hammer and sickle.

"Now let's go down to the end of this room, where the big map is framed. That's the earliest land lot map of Fulton County. Actually it is a wall map. I had it put under glass. Eighteen seventy-two, the date is. All the land lots, who owned them, etc., and the railroads.

"These are all books pertaining to the Civil War. I say Civil War, but sometimes say War Between the States. . . . Some of my older friends seem to favor that. John Ashley Jones . . . he contends it wasn't a civil war at all. I think the title's a little cumbersome.

"These shelves are devoted mostly to Atlanta and Georgia. There are many rare books here. Here are newspapers. I don't collect newspapers especially, but I had a chance to get these, so I picked them up. That's the first half of 1889. But I don't try. . . . Here are the censuses. . . . I have had them photostated and then bound in book form, numbered the pages. I have an index for each one, so we can find any given information without sitting in front of those machines. If you have those machines bright enough so you can see, they hurt your eyes.

"This is the Fulton County census of 1900, which is rather voluminous, but they have an index, so I can find a name anytime. Practically all the books in these revolving lawyers' bookcases are histories of Georgia counties or cities . . . Newton, Coweta, Elbert, Douglas, Fayette, Hapeville, etc. This file goes around and fits right under the stacks. I use this file frequently. Some of these county books are rare now. A good many genealogical books down below . . . and here's a set of the roster of the Confederate soldiers of Georgia, and that's very useful. You can find out when a man joined the army and all sorts of useful things about him. That's Butts County . . . and Cobb County.

"The Historical Society has most of these county histories. I'm not trying to get a complete set. I'm interested in the counties nearer Atlanta. Occasionally I am given one further away, and I am glad to have it. As you know, I am doing a necrology of Fulton and DeKalb Counties, so I am using these extensively . . . any newspaper, obits, cemetery records, etc. I do a lot of work with county records . . . inventories and appraisals of estates.

"For instance, Hardy Ivy didn't leave a will. He was thrown from a horse and killed in 1842, late in the year. So his administrator's bond was dated January 23, 1843. Sarah Ivy, administratrix, and William Ezzard finally took that over. But here is everything he had, with the value: brindle cow and yearling, $8; a pine table, 50¢; one sideboard and contents, $3; small bed and stead, $5; sad irons, $1; one lot of books, $3; one shotgun and pouch, $5. He didn't own any slaves apparently. A number of these estates did, and they were among the most valuable assets. . . .

"Here's one of Alston H. Green. I'll get that one out. . . .This man owned thirty-seven slaves. That was probably the largest slave holding in this immediate area. Now, Mr. Green's plantation was out there along the Chattahoochee River where the Charlie Brown Airport is now . . . around Gordon Street. This was Alston H. Green, DeKalb County (that was before Fulton County had been created).

"Able-bodied young men were much sought after. Alston Green would have been considered a pretty wealthy man. Here's a family cemetery. I was out there on November 7, 1930. What were you doing that day?

"And here, a W. A. Green, who was a member of the Green family, age twenty-six years, two months, and twenty-seven days . . . accidentally shot while bird hunting. That was information given to me by the Green family. That was not on a tombstone.

"Here is a McDonald family. 'Sacred to the memory of John McDonald, who departed this life after suffering excruciating pain for thirteen months, on July 30, 1853, age fifty-one years and twenty days.'

"It will take me at least five years to get my necrology finished. I enjoy doing it, and my reading program is suffering a bit when I work on this . . . but after all, I've been working on this a long time. I started gathering all this information in 1930. That is sixty-three years, as I figure it.

"I had to go to both courthouses, Fulton and DeKalb Counties. I expect to leave all this to the Historical Society, and I would hope they would be well taken care of. People are constantly making copies of pages out of books. It doesn't do the books a bit of good to be stretched out like that. . . . It's destructive. Breaks the spine and the head . . . well, it just hurts them.

"Anyway, my cemetery records are in twenty-two volumes. This is all part of the necrology, which is an Egyptian word meaning 'a list of the dead.'

"Here's a page I've filled out. I can't find everything about everybody, but I find as much as I can.

"This is the late Alex King, who was a senior partner in King and Spalding. Here is his father, J. Gadsden King, who was a major in the Confederate Army . . . where he was born, his birthdate, when he came to Atlanta, his parents, his wife's maiden name, what business he was in, where he lived, what public offices he held . . . death date, where he was buried . . . Civil War veteran. I am not trying to give a lot of statistics, and also he was president of the Atlanta Board of Underwriters in 1876.

"Here is Mitchell King. I believe he and his wife live in Hilton Head now. I liked Mitchell very much, and his wife is a great tennis player.

"Anyway, what I will do is make out one of these pages for every white male over twenty-one who ever lived in the county long enough not to be considered a transient. And these are my extracts from newspaper obits. . . . Here is the year 1906.

"I do these in pencil because I anticipate that they will be printed. Here are obit books, by years. They go back to 1857; keep them up through 1932. That's not all of them. There are some more. And some of them are over there. I haven't got the space here. And here are some miscellaneous family histories and information about people.

"And in all the drawers in here . . . some of them on that side and over here, are my railroad time table collections. This is a good way to keep them . . . fifteen drawers, large drawers.

"This table/file/desk is where I work, standing up (it is about elbow height). . . . Clem Ford designed this. He did like to stand up, and of course architects do have to have a wide base. . . . It is about ten feet by six feet. The railroad time tables I keep in these folders, and they are arranged by year. Here are the ones from the Baltimore and Ohio, dated from 1868–1910, one a year.

"My filing system . . . I know where everything is, and that is important. Because I work on this necrology. Now there are the death certificates from the city of Atlanta. You wouldn't have access to them now, but when I was doing it, you did. In fact, I doubt that most of our public officials would know where the record is.

"Now if a death is not natural, I record the cause. Let's see here, if I can find one . . . . Here's one 'gunshot in side,' there's another, 'gunshot in head.' . . .

"I found those on the death certificate. They are on those always . . . and in the obits. Most of the obits give the cause, but they are careful about reporting suicide.

"Here are many more books dealing with Georgia and Atlanta. Here is the *Georgia Historical Quarterly.* . . . I am missing two or three issues. Maybe they'll turn up later. Here are my city directories of Atlanta . . . all three of those shelves. . . . About fifteen feet of shelving, about five feet in height. They are full of city directories . . . arranged chronologically. The older ones are not as big as the later ones . . . but this is a complete set, and they're in their original bindings, for the most part . . . with the ads. Many of them contained full maps of the city . . . folded. So these gave occupations. Here's Caroline Little, widow of Benjamin. A street out on the south side is named for that family. Here's a fellow who was a mail clerk for the *Constitution*. Here's a printer for the *Constitution*. Here's a fellow who ran a saloon. Here's a lawyer, O. A. Lochrane. The Bryans are related to him.

"I think one of the handsomest monuments at Oakland Cemetery is that of O. A. Lochrane, who died in 1887.

"Here are some previous histories of Atlanta, including my own. And inside, this is my collection of early city directories for other major cities. Here's one, the New York City directory for 1798. I thought the next time I went to New York I'd check out some of these people.

"I think they have a set. I hope they do. Here's a well-known name: Alexander Hamilton, Counselor at Law, 26 Broadway. . . . Then they even have his nemesis . . . Aaron Burr . . . Counselor at Law, 55 Williams Street. That's quite a way out. Kind of hard to arrange a duel from there.

"Here's a Washington directory for 1863. We find here Abraham Lincoln, President of the United States, Executive Mansion, between 15th Street and streets west.

"I see here, John C. Calhoun, Secretary of War.

"Here's a city directory for Philadelphia in 1808. Can't overlook the date . . . it's very important. A lot of well-known people are listed here. Philadelphia, Washington, Boston . . . that's where the action was. Here's a first directory of Cincinnati. . . . I have had to have it bound. It never had a hard cover . . . 1821.

"You have to handle these things very carefully. . . . They call that 'foxing' as you probably know . . . those brown spots.

"This lacked a map, so I sent up to ask them to take a picture of their map, which they did and sent it back, and I bound it in this directory of mine.

"Here are some Baltimore directories in which my great-grandfather Kirkwood would be listed. These are getting more valuable all the time.

"This is a history of Atlanta that is getting pretty scarce. Frank Walsh . . . probably could get $250 for this one. Reed's *History of Atlanta*, 1889. The only pictures are steel engravings of prominent men. There is O. A. Lochrane, whom I have already mentioned. He was a little overweight. This book is gilt edged . . . they call it full gilt. That's Dr. Robert Ridley (I thought of growing some whiskers like that, but Frances vetoed it.)

"Here's a book written by Thomas H. Martin, who was secretary of the Chamber of Commerce for many years and later moved out to the Pacific Northwest. It's full of information, even though it is fairly chronological down to the Civil War. . . . Then it's departmentalized, a legal history. . . .

"He died, according to this obit, on June 4, 1936, in Tacoma, Washington, secretary of the Chamber of Commerce there. The obits should be recognized more than this. . . . He wrote two big books.

"Well, there are my city directories. You can see they're in good shape. They're not falling to pieces. Here's one I must take to the bindery and have it rebound. It's a nice rich cover . . . but it is coming loose. The bindery can repair this. We have a good bindery. The National Library Bindery is good, but it's a little inaccessible to me now. They are way up at Haynes Bridge Road in North Fulton. I usually go up there with the colonel. He binds things . . . Colonel Bogle.

"Now these photographs are of two of the best friends I ever had. . . . They're old enough to be my father. Of course, I had friends of my own age. That's Beverly DuBose, Sr., and Wilbur Kurtz, Sr.

"Here are histories of churches, and this contains information I have picked up here and there about Atlanta families. I use this quite often. This is an office file with four drawers . . . *fulllll*. I can squeeze something else in . . . maybe.

"Well, we've made a tour of the library. Let's go into the living room, where two walls are filled with books. . . .

"Most of the books with the handsome leather bindings are classical literature. Here we have *Lord Jim, Ivanhoe, Gulliver's Travels, Treasure Island, The Aenead, The Canterbury Tales, Mill on the Floss,* . . . magazines bound, *Antiques* . . . *Holiday,* when it was originally published. I thought *Holiday* was a very interesting magazine.

"Virginia Campbell Courts has been a good friend. She gave me this book. It has a rather interesting inscription: J. B. Campbell, . . . To Campbell Courts, January 4, 1970. This is a book about antique English furniture from Gothic to Sheraton.

Notes from an Interview with Virginia Campbell Courts
(Mrs. Richard W. Courts) on June 24, 1993

"Yes, Franklin and I have been good friends a long time. My father was very interested in history and I was formed in that frame of mind too.

"I didn't marry until quite late and Franklin was a bachelor too. So we dated. I remember that he used to pick me up, and we would drive out to Vinings Station . . . nothing there at that time but the Carters, and we would somberly watch the train coming down the tracks. The engineer knew Franklin and would always toot the horn.

"Then I would say, 'Now, Franklin, let's go see the oldest house you know.' We would find it, of course, probably an old derelict, and Franklin would see what looked to me like a pile of rocks. 'Now there,' he might have told me, 'was where an Irishman named . . . built that wall.'

"You have seen Franklin's wonderful library, organized, colorful, a perfect room for reading or study. Just what a library should be. One of his work stations is a table where he stands to work on his papers.

"My uncle, J. P. Stevens—Uncle Percy—who lived on Kimball Street, where the Fox Theatre is now, used to stand up to work too. He learned to read French (had never been to France, of course), standing up. I asked him why he did this, and he said, 'When I was a young man I did my reading and studying after a day at work. Unless I was standing up I would fall asleep.'"

——— — ———

"All of Thackeray's works are here. This is probably the best history of England. . . . *The Short History of the English People* . . . of course it is old now.

"Here are the *Life* magazine books on various American cities . . . a complete set of *Horizon* magazine. Here are some of these plates, in special niches.

"Up here is *Anna Karenina, War and Peace, The Origin of the Species* . . . I've read many of these, of course, but not all of them. But they are here, and I can always look forward to it.

"This is a set of books of the histories of famous museums. . . . There are thirty or so, published by *Time* and *Life*.

"This is the Hermitage in Leningrad . . . I love pretty pictures, I always have, . . . a Gainsborough . . . he painted beautiful women. Here are the treasures of the Smithsonian. Here is the baby bible in which our births are recorded, my sister and I, in our father's handwriting. I think my parents are in here too. Here's my mother, and there's my father. Katherine Kirkwood . . . my mother's maiden name. On February 17, 1889. Both of them died in March.

"Here in this big breakfront are more of the classics, and also the complete works of Prescott, and the *Georgia Historical Quarterly* beginning with the first year it was published. I am only missing two issues. When I get those, I will have them bound.

"Here's my first edition of *Gone with the Wind* complete with dust jacket and inscribed 'To Franklin Garrett with best regards and with great respect for his immense knowledge of Atlanta history, Margaret Mitchell.'

"I like that word 'immense.' It sounds so . . . immense. This is worth between $10,000 and $15,000, I think.

"And here is a nice edition of it, given to us by Penny and Bill Bohn. Penny was Penny Reinsch.

"And here is a copy of *Scarlett* inscribed to 'Franklin and Frances, with all good wishes, Alexandra Ripley.' Many people did prejudge that book. They wouldn't even listen to it being reviewed. It was well done . . . very well done.

"Here is *The Talisman* by Scott, Henry James's *Portrait of a Lady*, the poems of Keats, beautifully bound . . . *Twenty Thousand Leagues Under the Sea*, Homer's *Iliad*, *The Divine Comedy*. Over there we have the works of Plato, and *Uncle Tom's Cabin*, and works of Dickens, *Barnaby Rudge*. Here is a picture of Dickens in his studio.

"And the *Federalist Papers* and a fine copy of *Moby Dick* . . . and here is Huxley's *Brave New World*. I think this is a first edition of Mark Twain's *Life on the Mississippi*. Here are Cervantes' *Don Quixote* and *The Arabian Nights*, *The Rubaiyat*, Euripides. . . . I think when I go to my office tomorrow morning I'll ask the girl at the desk if Euripides had checked in yet.

"Here is *Washington and His Comrades in Arms*. I read that aloud when I was living alone, trying to improve my reading and speaking. The works of Montaigne . . . Virginia Courts gave me that too. I don't think there is any inscription in it. I enjoy having them all. It's a sort of a comfort to know they are here. . . .

"I have a complete set of *The American Heritage* . . . not all over here; a great number of these are in the bookcase over there . . . ."

The tape came to an end.

With the tape recorder whirring, Garrett sailed through his library almost casually, but that attitude belied his real appreciation for the volumes he has so carefully collected. Tucked into the flyleaves of many of the books are reviews, comments, and information pertaining to the author, indicating that Garrett is never finished with any of them. They are always in his mind.

In one book was a revealing quotation from Ralph Waldo Emerson: "Consider what you have in the smallest chosen library. A company of the wisest and wittiest men that could be picked out of all civilized countries, in a thousand years, have set in order the results of their learning and wisdom. The men themselves were hidden and inaccessible, solitary, impatient of interruption, fenced by etiquette; but the thought which they did not uncover to their bosom friend is here written out in transparent words to us, the strangers of another age."

And another snippet, somewhat wistful: "Next to acquiring good friends, the best acquisition is that of good books" — Colton.

After this interview was completed, the Atlanta History Center chose R. Carlisle Young to catalogue the Garrett library. The Garretts were delighted.

Young spent almost a year, parttime, putting the title pages of each book on a Library of Congress card, cross-referenced with the History Center catalogue. The library at the History Center is not computerized, but different collections are catalogued separately. Mr. Garrett's collection will be on a separate card system (as has been done for the DuBose and Shutze architectural collections). The cards will have the Library of Congress card above the name and above that the name of Garrett. "So that way you will have immediate access to the books," Young says.

"You know this library is Mr. Garrett's sanctuary." Carlisle Young comments. "I think Thomas Jefferson referred to his study as his sanctum sanctorum, and that is the way I feel about this room. Mr. Garrett comes home in the evening and spends hours in this library, working on his necrology or catching up on current periodicals he has received during the week. His devotion to scholarship is really remarkable. It really is.

"The Garretts love to share this room. When I came here to begin my work, Mr. Garrett walked over and pulled out a book that my grandfather had given to him in the mid-1950s, or late '40s. My grandfather was S. R. Young. He was president of the Georgia Railroad and the Atlanta and West Point Railroad and the Western Railroad of Alabama. Because of Mr. Garrett's fondness for everything about railroads, my grandfather and Mr. Garrett were natural friends."

Carlisle Young was surprised at the range of interests reflected in the books in the Garrett library. He asked Garrett whether it was a jump for him from Dickens to Georgia, or vice versa, and he replied, "It was no leap at all. I was always in another world."

But, continued Young, Garrett was very much in this world too. Every person, to him, has a richness of personality, and that's a lesson for historical societies. "The reason we are interested in history is that we are interested in the human parade."

1995

An Offer They Could Not Refuse

In the summer of 1995, when they were both in buoyant health, the Garretts, Franklin and Frances, received an offer they could not refuse.

They were given a unique gift, two burial plots in historic Oakland Cemetery against the day for their use. The famous Victorian cemetery, a stone's throw from downtown skyscrapers and rapid rail transit, has been the resting place for forty-eight thousand persons in its 146-year history. It has been closed to new interment since early in the 1950s. The gift to the Garretts seemed entirely appropriate to both groups involved, the cemetery officials and the Garrett family.

The famous cemetery is under the protection of the nonprofit Historic Oakland Foundation, which, from time to time, invites the interested public for an afternoon "Sunday in the Park" with the hope that the visitors will fall under its charms and will want to participate in its preservation.

At one recent Sunday afternoon reception, reenactors dressed themselves in mourning outfits and strolled around as docents, placed in the various areas of the cemetery—the black section, the Jewish section, the Civil War section—talked to people about the significance of those areas.

Franklin M. Garrett in Oakland Cemetery with two unidentified children, ca. 1995.
Jim Fitts, photographer. Photo courtesy of Franklin M. Garrett

Holly Crenshaw, staff writer for the *Atlanta Journal-Constitution*, wrote that three thousand people attended the autumn 1995 event, brought their picnic lunches, and seemed pleased to lend themselves to quiet reflection.

In a long article in the August 19, 1995, *Creative Loafing*, Garrett's well-established achievements as Atlanta's premier historian were recounted by Stephanie Ramage, who explained the circumstances of the burial plot bestowal.

Garrett, who in the past has written many corporate histories of Atlanta institutions, long ago wrote the official history of Oakland. He often brings visitors to Atlanta to the memorial, and has been photographed several times sitting on the granite boulder or a comfortable park chair telling stories to small spellbound children.

His favorite place, Stephanie Ramage wrote, is the Joseph E. Brown monument, "the one with the angel Gabriel who hasn't yet blown his horn, where MARTA flashes by and I can see the town. I've always thought that rather striking."

The incident of presenting the gift of the burial plots was explained by E. Allen Myers, Jr., the cemetery's sexton. "The city council had long ago named him the official historian of Atlanta, and it just made sense that he should be buried here with the people he has spent his life studying and writing about," Myers said.

Myers discovered a piece of ground near the entrance gate—the brick guard's booth—that seemed available. He had it "sounded" to be sure no one was buried there, and the Historic Oakland Foundation then paid the city for the plots.

Oakland's stately monuments, with fanciful spires and cupolas, gazebos and gothic mausoleums, have fascinated Atlantans and their visitors and have often been photographed and written about. In 1965 (that is thirty-one years ago), Norman Shavin, columnist for the *Atlanta Constitution* and himself an ardent historian, talked to Garrett about a marker to a bird . . . a mockingbird named "Tweetsie," buried in 1874.

The two men mentioned several inscriptions they had noticed especially, including this proud and defiant comment, "Confederate Soldier Unknown to Fame, Died for His Country All the Same."

Garrett observed to Shavin that Alexander Pope's immortal summation "An honest man is the noblest work of God" as often being inscribed, and another, "Mark the perfect man and behold the upright, for the end of that man is peace."

Of course Oakland has inscriptions to departed wives of wistful remembrance: "She had the honey of kindness, the salt of wit and the leaven of cheerfulness"; and another: "Beneath this stone doth lie/As much as virtue as could die/Which when alive did vigor give/To as much beauty as could live."

Then, quoting the Shavin column: "I asked Franklin if he had preplanned his own inscription, adding, 'I don't want to rush you,' to which he replied, 'No, I haven't . . . and I wouldn't cooperate with anyone trying to rush me into it.'"

CHAPTER 26

1996

Franklin's Portrait on the Wall of Fifteen-Story Carter Hall

The most spectacular public exposure Franklin Garrett has ever had was as one of the anchor portraits on the Coca-Cola Centennial Olympic Wall for the 1996 Olympic Games in Atlanta.

He was one of thirty-five outstanding Atlantans chosen to be included in a mosaic mural covering the north wall of the fifteen-story Carter Hall Building on Capitol Avenue, along the route of the Olympic flame and only a stone's throw from Olympic Stadium. Olympic visitors could not miss it.

The letter inviting him to accept this honor explained that "you have made a difference in the lives of others through hard work, dedication, love and understanding. Coca-Cola is proud to support those who strive to do their best . . . and your life exemplifies the best qualities of the Olympics ideals and spirit. Now we want to share your spirit with the world."

The mural as it was originally designed was to have forty faces on the mosaic, but Kevin E. Cole, the artist in charge of the project, said that the eighty-two thousand square-foot space lent itself more attractively to the lesser number. "Even though we had to put nine of these in the Coke bottle," which is the lightly suggested center of the wall painting.

Cole's work in developing the mosaic was a masterful piece of artistry . . . and engineering. With degrees from Northern Illinois University, the University of Illinois, and the University of Arkansas in the field of art and an admirable six-page résumé of art projects and commissions, he had never undertaken a project of such magnitude.

The individual portraits, which Cole prefers to call "interpretations of the spirit," were executed on vinyl panels with a special oil-based paint. He worked from photographs as well as personal sittings with each subject.

After Garrett's portrait had been elevated to its spot at the right-hand lower corner of the huge mural, someone jokingly remarked that he looked startled.

"I wasn't startled about the painting at all," Garrett replied. "I like it very much. So does my wife. But I was really startled when I watched them try to put it in place. The wind was blowing so hard they couldn't get the panels to behave, and they had to make three tries before it worked. They were working in a high wind on a high scaffold, and I just wonder how they got the ones at the top in place."

Cole explained that the vinyl was something like contact paper, which was already glued for use on the wall. "And happily, it worked."

The same day Garrett was recognized and feted with a luncheon to honor his acceptance, nine other outstanding persons were announced: Frederick Pitt Alderman, ninety, Georgia's oldest living gold medalist; the Rev. Samuel A. Alderman, pastor of the First Hispanic Baptist Church of Metro Atlanta; Elena Castro, a Houston County teacher who runs a baseball league for 162 special children; Rita Engelhardt, administrator of the City Catholic Colored Clinic in Buttermilk Bottom; Linda Fernee, recently named volunteer of the year by the Gwinnett County Community Council. Also Dr. Marvin C. Goldstein, a prominent Atlanta volunteer who opened the city's first free orthodontics clinic, and Thetus Allman Knox, Atlanta's first female police sergeant, lieutenant, and captain.

President Jimmy Carter and Rosalynn Carter were both included in the mosaic as well.

CHAPTER 27

1996

Two True Friends Keep Watch over Atlanta

Few left-at-home wives could assume, when their husbands jauntily set out together for a Saturday excursion, that the elderly gentlemen would spend their hours walking railroad tracks, climbing railroad embankments, or checking remote cemetery plots, but that has been the artless agenda that has faced the agreeable Mrs. Garrett and Mrs. James Bogle for many years of Saturdays on their own.

Since 1957, Garrett and Colonel Bogle (U.S. Army, retired) have also shared their fervent interest in reading, the collection of significant books, trains in all their embodiments, and the geographic and demographic decisions always being taken in burgeoning Atlanta.

The men, both certainly senior (Bogle is ten years Garrett's junior), have been friends, some say alter-egos, since Bogle bought two sets of Garrett's expansive *Atlanta and Environs*, one for his upstairs library, the other for his downstairs home office, and expressed to Garrett a deep interest in Atlanta's past and future.

They had met previously at the Civil War Round Table, which Franklin had himself initiated years earlier. Garrett then discovered that Bogle had been reared in Tennessee, the son of a railroad man, and

Franklin M. Garrett with Colonel James G. Bogle (U.S. Army, retired) walking the tracks at Howell Junction, 1993. Doris Lockerman, photographer. Photo courtesy of Franklin M. Garrett

that he had extensive knowledge and great interest in the Andrews Raid of Confederate fame.

James Bogle had married Mary Alice Clark in Atlanta in 1942 and had had several assignments in Atlanta in the military. Toward the time of their eventual retirement, the Bogle family had invested in a house in Atlanta to give their family a base and were in and out of the city frequently until his retirement from the army in 1967.

Over the years, Garrett and the colonel had worked out a neat schedule. Colonel Bogle had picked Garrett up at his home about midmorning on agreed Saturdays and they had skipped away for a hearty breakfast at the nearest Waffle House. They had previously decided, by telephone, which direction their day's rambling would take.

They took trails in and out of the city and in recent months poked around new venues for the upcoming summer Olympics. They often ran upon people who already knew them.

Bogle tells it: "We were going on the Southern line and a train was coming by. So we stood aside to get out of the way and look at the train, and as it went by a man hung out of the window of the engine and hollered: 'I know you, you're Franklin Garrett!' We never found out who he was . . . the train was going about a hundred miles an hour, but I thought it was unusual that he would stick his head out of the window and yell, 'I know you . . .'

"One of the nice things about being with Franklin is that there are always people who know him . . . recognize his name or his face, or his voice. He doesn't know them, of course; there is no way in the world for him to know all those people, but people speak to him.

"There are a lot of people interested in railroad history in Atlanta. We have a large chapter of the National Railway Historical Society here, about three or four hundred members. Franklin, incidentally, has been chairman of the board of the society since it has been around since 1959.

"The group has a railway museum called the Southeastern Railway Museum on Old Buford Highway, just south of Duluth, Georgia, where they have a circular track on a twelve-acre tract of land where they can operate a locomotive. They have had a diesel and a couple of cabooses behind it carrying people for the rides."

——— — ———

On December 7, 1991, the Atlanta chapter of the National Railway Historical Society, Inc., gave Franklin Garrett a certificate of appreciation with national and Atlanta life membership, in recognition of his having served as honorary chairman from January 1962 until December 1991.

——— — ———

"Everybody knows Franklin. People stop him at the museum and this lady or this man will say, 'Franklin Garrett, how nice to see you today,' or something pleasant. He always has time to stop, return the greeting, and engage in conversation, whatever the individuals want to talk about.

That, I think, is the remarkable trait that he has . . . he never sees a stranger.

"When we walk the railroad tracks, we obviously run into some dangerous-looking characters. We still speak, and we keep on walking. His association is with human beings, and very natural. He has no self-importance. He is always very friendly and is willing to give the other guy the benefit of the doubt.

"I am reminded of another comic situation. We had gone out to southeast Atlanta, not too far from Fort McPherson, to check on the grave of a Civil War soldier who was buried there. At this time it was in the rear of a liquor store, and at one side of the liquor store was an apartment building. Well, we drove out to the back and, sure enough, we ran into three or four men. One of them was working on an automobile. We explained what we wanted, and within about thirty seconds, we were the only ones left. They had all disappeared. . . . They weren't sure what we were up to.

"I told you we get breakfast somewhere, usually at a Waffle House. Well, sometimes we go back and get another waffle later . . . after a long tramp along the tracks, or a long ride into the country."

For his part, Garrett finds the colonel "easy to be with. He has a personality that is very pleasant. He doesn't constantly stir up the water . . . and of course we have an interest in trains and the railroads. He is a kindly man. We like the same things. We like to walk railroads. We're both familiar enough with them to know how to keep out of the way of trains. We don't get drunk and fall asleep on the tracks or anything like that.

"So anyway, we have many things we like to do together, books, walks, railroads. The colonel isn't interested in playing golf and neither am I, not that we don't like golf, but you can't do everything. Golf's a big time-taker, if there ever was one. We just enjoy being with each other.

"Mark Twain could have done something with this companionship . . . 'Life Along the Beltline,' perhaps."

CHAPTER 28

1996

Everything Seemed to Be in Order

In early March 1996, during a routine medical checkup, it was discovered that Garrett needed immediate attention for a hitherto unsuspected condition of the lungs. Thoracic surgery was indicated. He entered St. Joseph's Hospital on March 13 for a few days, as he expressed it.

No visitors. He had the constant encouragement of his wife, Frances, visits from his anxious son, Miller, and reassuring telephone conversations with his daughter, Patricia, from California. And outside, in the waiting room, his friends the Henry Howells, the Bogles, and one or two others, standing by.

Twenty days later, Garrett was back at Mainline, his surgery survived, back with Frances, his precious books, records, and Dollie, the couple's tiny "attack" Chihuahua.

On April 8, 1996, the *Wall Street Journal* published a front-page feature with a smiling picture of Garrett, calling him "A Walking History of Greater Atlanta." The article had obviously been prepared before his departure for the hospital, so no mention was made of that incident.

In a two-column review of Garrett's lifetime contributions, reporter Douglas A. Blackmon wrote that since the 1996 Olympics had been award-

Patricia Garrett Marshall and Miller Garrett, ca. 1980. Photo courtesy of Franklin M. Garret

ed to Atlanta, Mr. Garrett's encyclopedic memory had been in great demand.

The article commented: "He is often referenced in news accounts. In fact, more than eighty times in the last two years, in local newspapers."

The *Wall Street Journal's* man Mr. Blackmon was not aware that even more queries had come from national journals and broadcasters, and from television and radio news centers in Europe and other foreign countries where athletes, coaches, and fans were reserving space in Atlanta from which to observe the players and playing fields of the world in the summer of '96.

Garrett's habitual inspection of his city and its surrounding areas resumed. Within a few days, with his friend Jim Bogle at the wheel, they had inspected new developments at the Olympic sites, which were scattered all over Atlanta's environs as well as other communities in the area.

Since Garrett had arrived in Atlanta on the Royal Palm in May 1914 and adopted the city as his own, his "environs" had grown to more than 3,500,000 inhabitants before his very eyes. He had seen it all.

——— — ———

And everything seemed to be in order. But in railroad parlance — No Highballin' (which means going fast), No Open Throttle (which means going very fast), Just Hard Pullin', which everybody understands.

Hail or Farewell — a characteristic encounter with Franklin M. Garrett. Photo courtesy of the Atlanta History Center

Index